An Assessment of Two-Year Probationary Period Usage Within the Defense Civilian Workforce

A Report Prepared for the U.S. Department of Defense in Compliance with Section 1102 of the Fiscal Year 2020 National Defense Authorization Act

LAURA WERBER, JONAS KEMPF, MOLLY F. MCINTOSH, BRIAN PHILLIPS, SAMANTHA CHERNEY, DANIEL KIM

Prepared for the Office of the Under Secretary of Defense for Personnel and Readiness
Approved for public release; distribution unlimited

NATIONAL DEFENSE RESEARCH INSTITUTE

For more information on this publication, visit **www.rand.org/t/RRA667**-1.

About RAND

The RAND Corporation is a research organization that develops solutions to public policy challenges to help make communities throughout the world safer and more secure, healthier and more prosperous. RAND is nonprofit, nonpartisan, and committed to the public interest. To learn more about RAND, visit www.rand.org.

Research Integrity

Our mission to help improve policy and decisionmaking through research and analysis is enabled through our core values of quality and objectivity and our unwavering commitment to the highest level of integrity and ethical behavior. To help ensure our research and analysis are rigorous, objective, and nonpartisan, we subject our research publications to a robust and exacting quality-assurance process; avoid both the appearance and reality of financial and other conflicts of interest through staff training, project screening, and a policy of mandatory disclosure; and pursue transparency in our research engagements through our commitment to the open publication of our research findings and recommendations, disclosure of the source of funding of published research, and policies to ensure intellectual independence. For more information, visit www.rand.org/about/research-integrity.

RAND's publications do not necessarily reflect the opinions of its research clients and sponsors.

Published by the RAND Corporation, Santa Monica, Calif.
© 2023 RAND Corporation
RAND® is a registered trademark.

Library of Congress Cataloging-in-Publication Data is available for this publication.

ISBN: 978-1-9774-1170-9

Cover: *alexskopje - stock.adobe.com.*

About This Report

This report summarizes the results of a congressionally mandated independent review of the U.S. Department of Defense (DoD)'s use of the probationary period for new appointments to the Senior Executive Service and competitive service. The review was completed in the 2020-2021 time frame, with the draft final report submitted to DoD in February 2022. Before the results of RAND NDRI's independent review were submitted to DoD and Congress, Congress repealed the two-year probationary period in Section 1106 of the National Defense Authorization Act (NDAA) for fiscal year (FY) 2022. The effective date of the repeal was December 31, 2022. This report's publication was delayed as a result of the sponsor's prepublication and review processes.

Overall, this report covers the required report elements listed in Section 1102 of the NDAA for FY 2020. Findings address the composition of the workforce on probation and those terminated during their probationary periods; patterns in probationary period removals and disciplinary actions; concerns and promising practices related to the probationary period; and perceptions regarding the impact of an extended probationary period on employee recruiting and retention and DoD effectiveness. The report also includes recommendations intended to improve how DoD makes use of the probationary period and continues to assess its impact. This research should be of interest to congressional representatives and staff, DoD personnel involved with civilian personnel management and oversight, and to the broader community interested in federal civilian personnel management. Some expertise about federal civil service and government civilian personnel management is presumed.

National Security Research Division

This research was sponsored by the Office of the Under Secretary of Defense for Personnel and Readiness and conducted within the Personnel, Readiness, and Health Program of the RAND National Security Research Division (NSRD), which operates the National Defense Research Institute (NDRI), a federally funded research and development center sponsored by the Office of the Secretary of Defense, the Joint Staff, the Unified Combatant Commands, the Navy, the Marine Corps, the defense agencies, and the defense intelligence enterprise.

For more information on the RAND Personnel, Readiness, and Health Program, see www.rand.org/nsrd/prh or contact the director (contact information is provided on the webpage).

Acknowledgments

We appreciate the research sponsorship of the Department of Defense Assistant Secretary of Defense for Civilian Personnel Policy. We also benefited from the support of Brian Friedrich and Amy Stone, Defense Civilian Personnel Advisory Service, who served as our action officers.

In addition, we thank Scott Seggerman, Defense Manpower Data Center (DMDC), who prepared the DMDC data files that were central to RAND's analysis, transferred RAND's analysis file to DCPAS, and responded to many questions regarding the DMDC data.

RAND study team members interviewed subject-matter experts and supervisors whose participation, time, and insights are much appreciated. They are not identified here to protect their confidentiality.

Finally, we benefited from the contributions of our RAND colleagues. Jennifer Lewis and Ginger Groeber provided formal peer reviews that ensured our work meets RAND's standards for high quality research. Craig Bond and Daniel Ginsberg also offered constructive feedback on earlier versions of this report. Elizabeth Roth, Stephanie Williamson, and Christine DeMartini provided programming support. We thank them all, but we retain full responsibility for the objectivity, accuracy, and analytic integrity of the work presented here.

Summary

Issue

Poor employee performance and employee misconduct are important workforce management issues for the U.S. Department of Defense (DoD) to address given both their prevalence and potential impact on productivity. In light of the resources required to remove an individual with full employment rights from civil service, the probationary period for someone with a new civil service appointment is regarded as both the final step in the hiring process and an important tool for supervisors to address poor performance and misconduct

To facilitate effective use of this tool, in the National Defense Authorization Act (NDAA) for fiscal year (FY) 2016, Congress extended the probationary period from one to two years for individuals who were appointed to permanent positions in the competitive service and those who received career appointments in the Senior Executive Service (SES) on or after November 26, 2015.[1] Several years later, in Section 1102 of the NDAA for FY 2020, Congress directed the Secretary of Defense to conduct an independent review of how it had used that discretion (see Box S.1 for the Section 1102 text that outlines the required report elements).[2] DoD tasked RAND's National Defense Research Institute (NDRI), a federally funded research and development center, to conduct the review, and this report summarizes the results of that review.

Before the results of RAND NDRI's independent review were submitted to DoD and Congress, Congress repealed the two-year probationary period in Section 1106 of NDAA for FY 2022. The repeal went into effect December 31, 2022.

Approach

To carry out the independent review mandated by Congress and develop actionable recommendations for DoD, we used qualitative and quantitative methods. We relied most heavily on statistical analysis of Defense Manpower Data Center (DMDC) civilian personnel data files for personnel with a new SES or competitive service appointment between November 26, 2015, and December 31, 2018. We also conducted 31 interviews with DoD human resources (HR), legal, and Equal Employment Opportunity (EEO) professionals; DoD supervisors; and representatives from both employee unions and a manager association. In addition, we completed an in-depth review of case records for 43 probationary period removals. Finally, we reviewed Office of Special Counsel (OSC) and DoD EEO appeals data provided by our sponsor office.

Key Findings

The following report highlights are arranged to correspond to the required report elements. This section also includes concluding remarks about whether the second year of probation was helpful to DoD or detrimental to personnel.

---

[1] Public Law 114–92, National Defense Authorization Act for Fiscal Year 2016, November 25, 2015.

[2] Public Law 116–92, National Defense Authorization Act for Fiscal Year 2020, December 20, 2019.

BOX S.1

FY 2020 NDAA Section 1102: Report on the Probationary Period for Department of Defense Employees

(a) REPORT.—Not later than 1 year after the date of the enactment of this Act, the Secretary of Defense shall—

(1) conduct an independent review on the probationary periods applicable to Department of Defense employees under section 1599e of title 10, United States Code; and (2) submit a report on such review to the Committees on Armed Services and Oversight and Reform of the House of Representatives and the Committees on Armed Services and Homeland Security and Governmental Affairs of the Senate.

b) CONTENTS.—The review and report under sub section (a) shall cover the period beginning on the date of the enactment of such section 1599e and ending on December 31, 2018, and include the following:

(1) An assessment and identification of the demographics of each Department of Defense employee who, during such period, was on a probationary period and who was removed from the civil service, subject to any disciplinary action (up to and including removal), or who filed a claim or appeal with the Office of Special Counsel or the Equal Employment Opportunity Commission.

(2) A statistical assessment of the distribution patterns with respect to any removal from the civil service during such period of, or any disciplinary action (up to and including a removal) taken during such period against, any Department employee while the employee was on a probationary period.

(3) An analysis of the best practices and abuses of discretion by supervisors and managers of the Department with respect to probationary periods.

(4) An assessment of the utility of the probationary period prescribed by such section 1599e on the successful recruitment, retention, and professional development of civilian employees of the Department, including any recommendation for regulatory or statutory changes the Secretary determines to be appropriate.

(5) A discussion of the cases where the Department made a determination to remove a Department employee during the second year of such employee's probationary period.

(6) A summary of how the Department has implemented the authority provided in such section 1599e with respect to probationary periods, including the number, and a demographic summary, of each Department employee removed from the civil service, subject to any disciplinary action (up to and including removal), or who filed a claim or appeal with the Office of Special Counsel or the Equal Employment Opportunity Commission during the second year of any such employee's probationary period.

(c) CONSULTATION.—The analysis and recommendations in the report required under subsection (a) shall be prepared in consultation with Department of Defense employees and managers, labor organizations representing such employees, staff of the Office of Special Counsel and the Equal Employment Opportunity Commission, and attorneys representing Department employees in wrongful termination actions.

SOURCE: Public Law 116–92, 2019.

FY 2020 NDAA Section 1102 Report Elements 1 and 6 (Number and Demographics of Those Removed from the Civil Service, Subject to Disciplinary Action, or Who Filed a Claim or Appeal with the OSC or the EEOC [Equal Employment Opportunity Commission] During the Second Year of Probation)

- During the time frame of interest (November 26, 2015, through December 31, 2018), there were 164,694 personnel with a new competitive service appointment and 275 personnel with a new SES appointment.
- Those personnel tended to be male, White, non-Hispanic, and in positions covered by a bargaining unit. Looking at other protected classes, 47 percent of those on probation were age 40 or older, 51 percent were veterans, and 18 percent had a disability on record. In addition, the majority of those on probation (59 percent) were not in mission critical occupations (MCOs) or in science, technology, engineering, or mathematics (STEM) occupations. The U.S. Navy employed the largest share of those on probation, 33 percent, with the U.S. Army relatively close behind. At the subagency level, U.S. Army Medical Command and U.S. Air Force Materiel Command employed the largest shares of those on probation at 10 percent and 8 percent, respectively.
- Less than 1 percent of those personnel (1,304) were subject to disciplinary action in the form of a suspension during their probationary period, and 2.1 percent of those personnel (3,492) were terminated during their probationary period.[3] Forty-eight percent of those probationary period terminations occurred in the second or third year of employment.
- The Office of Special Counsel reviewed records for approximately 169,976 DoD probationary period employees and reported 259 appeals filed during the probationary period during the time frame of interest, including 143 during the second year of probation and 52 related to termination.
- Most DoD EEO offices did not provide appeals data for this study. The offices that did provide data only represent a very small percentage of probationary period personnel. Data limitations prevented us from calculating the number of probationary period personnel employed within those offices.[4] Together, those offices, all within DoD's Fourth Estate,[5] reported 39 appeals filed during the probationary period, including 11 filed during the second year and 25 related to terminations.

FY 2020 NDAA Section 1102 Report Element 2 (Patterns in Removals and Disciplinary Actions)

We used regression analysis to identify patterns related to three outcomes: termination during the probationary period, disciplinary action (i.e., suspension) during the probationary period, and probationary period terminations after the first year. It is important to note that the results are not causal, meaning that we cannot conclude that changing the probationary period length caused certain personnel to be terminated more or

---

[3] Fourteen personnel were both subject to disciplinary action and then later terminated during their probationary periods.

[4] The DMDC data files we used for our analysis do not include separate values for two of the nine DoD subagencies whose EEO offices submitted appeals data. This means we were unable to calculate either the number of covered personnel or the number of probationary period terminations associated with those subagencies. Looking at the seven subagencies included in the DMDC data files, together they include 2,350 covered personnel (less than 1 percent of all covered personnel) and 40 terminations (less than 1 percent of probationary period terminations during the time frame of interest). The entire Fourth Estate includes 26,284 (16 percent) of covered personnel and 729 (21 percent) of probationary period terminations.

[5] The *Fourth Estate* is a term used to refer to the Office of the Secretary of Defense, defense agencies, and defense field activities outside of the three military departments and the unified combatant commands (Kathleen J. McInnis, *Defense Primer: The Department of Defense*, Washington, D.C.: Congressional Research Service, last updated November 8, 2021).

less frequently. Instead, the results mean that, after taking observable factors into account, certain characteristics are correlated with being terminated or disciplined during one's probationary period. Tables S.1 and S.2 summarize the statistically significant factors related to a higher or lower probability of termination or disciplinary action compared with a referent group.[6] Table S.1 shows the intersection of findings related to probationary period terminations and disciplinary actions. For example, women were less likely than men to either be terminated or disciplined, and personnel aged 40 or older were less likely to be terminated than personnel younger than age 40, but there was no significant relationship between age and the probability of disciplinary action. Table S.2 shows the intersection related to probationary period terminations overall and after the first year in particular (conditional on being terminated). For example, none of the personal, organizational, and occupational factors in the regression models were significantly associated with a higher probability of both probationary period termination and termination after the first year of probation. In the tables, shading is used to highlight the factors that were statistically significant for both outcomes.

Turning first to the comparison of probationary period termination and probationary period disciplinary action findings (Table S.1), we note that some factors are statistically correlated with a higher probability of both termination and disciplinary action. For example, Black personnel and bargaining unit members are more likely to be terminated and disciplined. Conversely, there are factors statistically associated with a lower probability of both outcomes. Examples include those with at least a bachelor's degree, and those in STEM occupations, whether mission critical or not.

It is helpful to consider what might be driving these findings, in part because different reasons might suggest the need for different responses. For example, for people with at least a bachelor's degree, it is plausible that additional education is correlated with better performance, which reduces the probability of termination or disciplinary action. Another hypothesis is that STEM personnel are in high demand and difficult to recruit, so there may be a reluctance to use any sort of formal adverse action for these employees. Finally, there are two instances in which the significance of outcomes was in the opposite direction: (1) the probability of termination was lower for those in the HR Management occupation, but the probability of disciplinary action was higher, and (2) conversely, for those working at the Defense Commissary Agency, the probability of a probationary period termination was higher, but the probability of probationary period disciplinary action was lower. The latter case may reflect an organizational practice not to use suspensions (our measure of disciplinary actions) with probationary employees.

Looking next at Table S.2, many factors were significantly associated with a higher probability of termination—including having a disability, working in one of seven Navy subagencies (e.g., Naval Air Systems Command, U.S. Marine Corps), and being a nurse—but few of them were also significantly associated with a higher probability of termination after the first year. Higher education was again significantly correlated with two outcomes. In this case, having some college or a higher level of education was statistically associated with a lower probability of probationary period termination but, conditional on being terminated, a higher probability of being terminated after the first year. One possible explanation for this aspect is that if, in general, those with more education have a higher level of performance, so supervisors may be giving personnel with more education the benefit of the doubt and waiting until the second year to initiate a termination.

---

[6] Statistically significant results are significant at *p*-value < .05

TABLE S.1
Summary of Probationary Period Termination and Probationary Period Disciplinary Action Patterns

	Probability of Probationary Period Disciplinary Action		
Probability of probationary period termination	**Lower and Significant**	**Higher and Significant**	**Not Significant**
Lower and significant	**Personal attribute** • Female • Bachelor's degree or higher **Service, component, or agency** • Defense Contract Management Agency **Occupation** • MCO/STEM • Non-MCO/STEM • Economist • Mechanical Eng • Misc Clerk and Assistant	**Occupation** • HR Mgmt	**Personal attribute** • Age 40 and older • Asian race • Hispanic ethnicity • Veteran • Some college • Mid-level pay grade at entry • Senior-level pay grade at entry **Service, component, or agency** • Air Force • Army • Navy • Army National Guard units (Title 32) **Location** • Hawaii Locality Pay Area (LPA) **Occupation** • MCO/non-STEM • Contracting • Education and Training Technician • Financial Admin and Program • Fire Protection and Prevention • General Business and Industry • Logistics Mgmt; Security Admin
Higher and significant	**Service, component, or agency** • Defense Commissary Agency	**Personal attribute** • Black • Bargaining unit **Service, component, or agency** • Air Force Materiel Cmd • U.S. Army Reserve Cmd • U.S. Fleet Forces Cmd • U.S. Pacific Fleet	**Personal attribute** • American Indian or Alaska Native • Other race • Disability **Service, component, or agency** • Air Combat Cmd • Army Corps of Engineers • Army Medical Cmd • Naval Air Systems Cmd • Naval Facilities Engineering Cmd
Not significant	**Occupation** • IT Mgmt	**Personal attribute** • Supervisor **Location** • Boston LPA **Occupation** • Inventory Mgmt	**Service, component, or agency** • Naval Medical Cmd • Navy Installations Cmd • U.S. Marine Corps • DoD Education Activity **Occupation** • Misc Warehousing and Stock Handling • Nurse All other personal, organizational, and occupational factors in the regression models

SOURCE: Authors' analysis of DMDC data.

NOTES: Statistically significant results are significant at p-value < .05. Referent groups include male, younger than age 40, White race, no college, non-Hispanic ethnicity, no known disability, non-veteran, not being a bargaining unit member, entry-level pay grade at entry, Fourth Estate, and, for occupation group, non-MCO/non-STEM. For LPA, agency, and specific occupations, the referent group is all others. The Accounting occupation was associated with a significantly higher probability of termination but dropped out of disciplinary actions models because of multicollinearity. The table does not include significant findings for unnamed occupations or "missing" categories. Shading is used to highlight the factors that were statistically significant for both outcomes. Admin = Administration; Cmd = Command; Eng = Engineering; IT = Information Technology; Mgmt = Management; Svcs = Services.

TABLE S.2
Summary of Probationary Period Termination and Probationary Period Termination Timing Patterns

		Probability of probationary period termination after first year, conditional on being terminated		
		Lower and significant	**Higher and significant**	**Not significant**
Probability of probationary period termination	**Lower and significant**	None of the personal, organizational, and occupational factors included in the regression models	**Personal attribute** • Some college • Bachelor's degree or higher **Service, component, or agency** • Army National Guard units (Title 32) **Location** • Hawaii LPA **Occupation** • MCO/non-STEM • Logistics Mgmt	**Occupation** • MCO/STEM • Non-MCO/STEM • Contracting • Economist • Education and Training Technician • Financial Admin and Program • Fire Protection and Prevention • General Business and Industry • HR Mgmt • Mechanical Eng • Misc Clerk and Assistant • Security Admin **Personal attribute** • Age 40 and older • Female • Asian race • Hispanic ethnicity • Veteran • Mid-level pay grade at entry • Senior-level pay grade at entry **Service, component, or agency** • Air Force • Army • Navy • Defense Contract Mgmt Agency
	Higher and significant	**Service, component, or agency** • Defense Commissary Agency • DoD Education Activity	None of the personal, organizational, and occupational factors included in the regression models	**Service, component, or agency** • Naval Air Systems Cmd • Naval Facilities Engineering Cmd • Naval Medical Cmd • Navy Installations Cmd • U.S. Fleet Forces Cmd • Marine Corps • U.S. Pacific Fleet **Occupation** • Accounting • Misc Warehousing and Stock Handling • Nurse **Personal attribute** • Black • American Indian or Alaska Native • Other race • Disability • Bargaining unit **Service, component, or agency** • Air Combat Cmd • Air Force Materiel Cmd • Army Corps of Engineers • Army Medical Cmd • Army Reserve Cmd
	Not significant	**Occupation** • Sales Store Clerical	**Service, component, or agency** • Defense Finance and Accounting Svcs • Defense Logistics Agency	All other personal, organizational, and occupational factors included in the regression models

SOURCE: Authors' analysis of DMDC data.

NOTES: Statistically significant results are significant at p-value < .05. Referent groups include male, younger than age 40, White race, no college, non-Hispanic ethnicity, no known disability, non-veteran, not being a bargaining unit member, entry-level pay grade at entry, Fourth Estate, and, for occupation group, non-MCO/non-STEM. For LPA, agency, and specific occupations, the referent group is all others. Army National Guard units (Title 32) were associated with a significantly lower probability of termination timing models due non probationary period terminations beyond first year. The table does not include significant findings for unnamed occupations or "missing" categories. Shading is used to highlight the factors that were statistically significant for both outcomes. Admin = Administration; Cmd = Command; Eng = Engineering; IT = Information Technology; Mgmt = Management; Svcs = Services.

FY 2020 NDAA Section 1102 Report Element 5 (Discussion of Cases in Which DoD Made a Determination to Remove an Individual During the Second Year of Probation)

- In most cases that resulted in terminations within the first year, reasons for termination are relatively clear cut (e.g., performance, attendance, or conduct issues that quickly arose) and, compared with later terminations, there were less documentation of feedback and warnings over time. For terminations that occurred in the second year, they involved probationary employees in their positions for more than one year but were terminated because of a specific incident (e.g., threat, forgery, failed drug test) or those with ongoing performance or misconduct issues that ultimately led to their terminations.
- There did not appear to be much difference between first- and second-year terminations with respect to documented supervisor dialogue with leadership or others prior to terminating the individual, or whether there was ever any documented positive feedback to the probationary employee (uncommon in general).
- There were few obvious cases of probationary employees terminated in the second year of probation for performance reasons that would have been difficult to observe in the first year because of extensive employee training and rotational requirements. Among the limited set of cases we reviewed, it typically did not appear to be the case that the nature of the work being performed over the first year differed from the long-term nature of the role (e.g., if it were limited to training assignments).

FY 2020 NDAA Section 1102 Report Elements 3 and 4 (Analysis of Best Practices and Abuses of Discretion and Assessment of the Probationary Period's Utility for Recruiting, Retention, and Professional Development)

- Based on the data sources analyzed, we did not find evidence of abuse of discretion by supervisors with respect to probationary periods. We could also not conclude that such abuse or discrimination was not occurring, but DoD organizations have processes in place to ensure that terminations are for appropriate reasons.
- Supervisors were noted as, at times, falling short in their use of the probationary period as a tool because they did not sufficiently communicate with probationary employees about performance or conduct issues prior to initiating a termination. Some were also perceived as waiting until probation was very close to ending before that initiation.
- Process-related concerns were linked to probationary period length computations, supervisor notification of probationary period end dates, and variation in the appeals rights documentation provided to terminated probationary employees.
- Promising practices include push notifications to supervisors via email notification or HR communication regarding upcoming probation end dates; documentation in termination case records of incidents and communications during a probationary employee's tenure that later help establish that a termination was for appropriate reasons; use of a termination checklist to navigate supervisors through the process; and use of an agency chain of command–based expedited process for terminated individual to request review.
- Evidence regarding the impact of the probationary period on recruiting and retention was limited. The interviewees who discussed this issue tended to believe that it did not influence recruiting or retention, and they did not offer opinions about its effect on professional development.

Concluding Observations

We are unable to conclude whether extending the probationary period from one year to two years for newly appointed SES and competitive service personnel was beneficial to DoD or detrimental to DoD personnel. To do so, we would need to analyze probationary period terminations and disciplinary actions both before the two-year probationary period went into effect and after, but our request for administrative data prior to 2015 was declined. This type of analysis would have helped us to evaluate whether the extended probation was working as intended (i.e., by giving supervisors more time to assess employees whose jobs require it) and to consider whether the higher probability of probationary termination for protected classes, such as Black personnel and those with a disability (which was found in the current analysis) was also present when the probation length was one year. In addition, the extended probationary period was in effect for a relatively short period of time. To understand how a longer probationary period influences recruiting, career development, and retention, analysis over a longer time frame, and, ideally, including the perspectives of employees, is needed. Finally, it was outside our study scope to assess whether the extra year of probation enabled some probationary employees to improve their performance or conduct and thereby avoid termination. Given the costs and time required to hire quality personnel, averted terminations is another important outcome to measure when evaluating the benefits of longer probation.

Recommendations

The report includes seven recommendations intended to improve DoD's use of the probationary period as the final stage of its hiring process. Given the decentralized way that HR matters are handled within the department, a combination of organizations, including Defense Civilian Personnel Advisory Service; the Office for Diversity, Equity, and Inclusion; and service- or component-level organizations (e.g., U.S. Army Civilian Human Resources Agency, Department of the Navy Office of Civilian Human Resources), will need to be involved in considering and implementing these recommendations.

- **Investigate higher termination rates for protected classes:** Especially in light of DoD's commitment to make the department "a workplace of choice that is characterized by diversity, equality, and inclusion,"[7] it is critical that the department develop, communicate, and implement plans to investigate these higher termination rates and to address any situations in which it finds that a termination did not seem to be for a valid reason. Involvement of key diversity, equity, and inclusion stakeholders and representatives from unions with rights to participate in a process of this nature could help ensure that such efforts are perceived as transparent and fair.
- **Conduct additional research to understand the benefits and shortcomings of a longer probationary period:** Looking at probation terminations before the two-year probationary period went into effect and a look over a longer time frame would help DoD better understand the impact of the extended probationary period. Such efforts will show how the extended time influenced retention and whether the termination patterns we found in this study persist over time. Other promising lines of inquiry include examining cases in which probationary employees turned their performances around in the second year, collecting information directly from prospective and current employees, and assessing how Science and Technology Reinvention Laboratory demonstration projects have used extended probation for certain personnel.

---

[7]   The department's full diversity, equity, and inclusion statement and a list of related initiatives is available online (see DoD, Office for Diversity, Equity, and Inclusion, homepage, undated).

- **Improve performance ratings recordkeeping:** A lack of performance ratings data prevented us from examining the link between poor performance and probationary period termination. As DoD continues to improve its approach to performance management and invest in its HR data systems, it should ensure that performance ratings are part of all civilian personnel employment records.

- **Increase the accuracy of probationary period end date computations:** Errors in these computations are too common according to our interviewees and their consequences great. Accordingly, efforts to reduce these errors, such as not computing end dates without full documentation, centralizing these computations, and audits or spot checks, are warranted.

- **Use push notifications to remind supervisors of probationary period end dates:** Supervisors' lack of awareness of probationary period end dates is a long-standing concern, which parts of DoD are trying to address via various push notification practices. These efforts should be extended departmentwide.

- **Consider broader application of termination promising practices:** Our analysis revealed promising practices related to push notifications and the handling of termination cases, such as documentation of feedback, use of a termination checklist, and an option for the employee being terminated to request expedited review within an agency's chain of command of the pending termination action. These practices all may improve the efficiency and effectiveness of the use of the probationary period and thus are candidates for broader application.

- **Look to the private sector for promising practices related to termination:** Private sector organizations have limits in some contexts on at-will employment (e.g., the implied contract exception) and have other reasons to ensure that terminations are both timely and appropriate. Accordingly, these organizations, particularly those with large, diverse workforces in multiple states, may be an additional source of promising practices for DoD to consider.

Contents

Boxes and Tables

Boxes

Tables

CHAPTER ONE

Introduction and Approach

Study Background

Use of the Probationary Period in Defense Civilian Personnel Management

Poor employee performance and employee misconduct are important workforce management issues for the U.S. Department of Defense (DoD) to address given both their prevalence and potential impact on productivity. In a 2016 Merit Systems Protection Board (MSPB) survey, 25 percent of DoD supervisors indicated that they supervise one or more poor performers. Moreover, roughly 60 percent of these supervisors agreed that a poor performer would negatively affect the other subordinates' ability to do their own jobs, and 90 percent believed that other subordinates' morale would wane if a supervisor failed to address poor performance.[1]

The probationary period provides a way for DoD to address efficiently the problems of poor performance and misconduct for individuals with a new competitive service appointment or Senior Executive Service (SES) appointment. Specifically, this final step in the hiring process gives supervisors a chance to assess an individual's performance and determine whether an appointment to the civil service should become final. Terminating an individual before his or her probationary period ends is a less onerous process for DoD than post-probation because the department does not have to follow the formal procedures enumerated in either 5 U.S. Code (U.S.C.) Section 4303 or 5 U.S.C. Section 7513, and the individual's appeal rights are limited.[2] Aware of these advantages, the Office of Personnel Management (OPM) urges supervisors in its guide on addressing and resolving poor performance[3] that they make full use of the probationary period, and DoD expresses similar sentiments in its supervisor guide on addressing employee performance issues early.[4]

Despite these benefits and encouragement, research indicates that DoD supervisors at times fall short in terminating poorly performing individuals before their probationary periods end. For example, in a 2015 report, the U.S. Government Accountability Office (GAO) described concerns that a supervisor failed to terminate a poor performer during his or her probationary period because the supervisor did not realize the individual's probationary period was ending.[5] In other cases, supervisors did not decide on an individual's continued service with the organization because they had insufficient time to gauge the individual's performance in all aspects of the job.

---

[1] Laura Werber, Paul W. Mayberry, Mark Doboga, and Diana Gehlhaus, *Support for DoD Supervisors in Addressing Poor Employee Performance: A Holistic Approach*, Santa Monica, Calif.: RAND Corporation, RR-2665-OSD, 2018.

[2] 5 U.S.C. Section 4303, Actions Based on Unacceptable Performance, January 3, 2012; and 5 U.S.C. Section 7513, Cause and Procedure, January 7, 2011.

[3] OPM, "Addressing and Resolving Poor Performance: A Guide for Supervisors," March 2017.

[4] DoD, Defense Civilian Personnel Advisory Service (DCPAS), "Addressing Performance Issues Early," webpage, undated.

[5] Robert Goldenkoff, *Federal Workforce: Improved Supervision and Better Use of Probationary Periods Are Needed to Address Substandard Employee Performance*, Washington, D.C.: U.S. Government Accountability Office, GAO-15-191, February 2015.

Congressional Attention to DoD's Use of the Probationary Period

Perhaps in recognition of perceived benefits of the probationary period and reports that one year was not always sufficient for a full evaluation, Congress turned its attention to this aspect of defense workforce management in 2015. Specifically, in Section 1105 of the National Defense Authorization Act (NDAA) for fiscal year (FY) 2016, Congress amended 10 U.S.C. by adding Section 1599e.[6] This new section required that the appointment of *covered employees* within DoD become final only after the individual completed a two-year probationary period. Covered employees include individuals who were appointed to permanent positions in the competitive service and those who received career appointments in the SES within DoD on or after November 26, 2015. In a September 27, 2016, DoD memorandum, the acting Deputy Assistant Secretary of Defense for Civilian Personnel Policy announced this change in the statute governing the probationary period, indicating that it went into effect November 26, 2015.[7]

A few years later, in Section 1102 of the NDAA for FY 2020, Congress directed the Secretary of Defense to conduct an independent review of the probationary periods applicable to DoD employees under 10 U.S.C. 1599e.[8] The Act states that the review should cover the period beginning on the date of the enactment of Section 1599e (November 26, 2015) and ending on December 31, 2018, and lists specific items to address in the review, including demographics of those on probation and terminated during their probation; patterns in probationary period terminations; misuse and best practices associated with the probationary period; and effects on recruiting, career development, and retention (see Box 1.1. for the Section 1102 text that outlines the required report elements). DoD tasked the RAND Corporation's National Defense Research Institute (NDRI), a federally funded research and development center, to conduct the review, and this report summarizes the results of that review.

At the time of this report's writing, before the results of our independent review were submitted to DoD and Congress, lawmakers repealed the two-year probationary period in Section 1106 of NDAA for FY 2022. The repeal goes into effect December 31, 2022.

Research Approach

RAND NDRI conducted an independent review in the 2020–2021 time frame. Work commenced in July 2020 and the draft final report was initially planned to be submitted to DoD in November 2021. However, after a delay in receipt of Equal Employment Opportunity (EEO) data from DoD, RAND NDRI and DoD agreed to extend the study for various DoD EEO offices to compile the requested EEO data. Ultimately, the draft final report was submitted to DoD in February 2022. Before the results of RAND NDRI's independent review were submitted to Congress and DoD, Congress repealed the two-year probationary period in Section 1106 of NDAA for FY 2022. The repeal went into effect December 31, 2022.

---

[6] Public Law 114–92, National Defense Authorization Act for Fiscal Year 2016, November 25, 2015; 10 U.S.C. Section 1599e, Probationary Period for Employees, January 6, 2017.

[7] The full memorandum is available online (see Office of the Assistant Secretary of Defense, Deputy Assistant Secretary of Defense for Civilian Personnel Policy, "Subject: Probationary Period for New Employees," memorandum, Washington, D.C., September 27, 2016).

[8] Public Law 116–92, National Defense Authorization Act for Fiscal Year 2020, December 20, 2019.

BOX 1.1

FY 2020 NDAA Section 1102: Report on the Probationary Period for Department of Defense Employees

(a) REPORT.—Not later than 1 year after the date of the enactment of this Act, the Secretary of Defense shall—

(1) conduct an independent review on the probationary periods applicable to Department of Defense employees under section 1599e of title 10, United States Code; and (2) submit a report on such review to the Committees on Armed Services and Oversight and Reform of the House of Representatives and the Committees on Armed Services and Homeland Security and Governmental Affairs of the Senate.

b) CONTENTS.—The review and report under sub section (a) shall cover the period beginning on the date of the enactment of such section 1599e and ending on December 31, 2018, and include the following:

(1) An assessment and identification of the demographics of each Department of Defense employee who, during such period, was on a probationary period and who was removed from the civil service, subject to any disciplinary action (up to and including removal), or who filed a claim or appeal with the Office of Special Counsel or the Equal Employment Opportunity Commission.

(2) A statistical assessment of the distribution patterns with respect to any removal from the civil service during such period of, or any disciplinary action (up to and including a removal) taken during such period against, any Department employee while the employee was on a probationary period.

(3) An analysis of the best practices and abuses of discretion by supervisors and managers of the Department with respect to probationary periods.

(4) An assessment of the utility of the probationary period prescribed by such section 1599e on the successful recruitment, retention, and professional development of civilian employees of the Department, including any recommendation for regulatory or statutory changes the Secretary determines to be appropriate.

(5) A discussion of the cases where the Department made a determination to remove a Department employee during the second year of such employee's probationary period.

(6) A summary of how the Department has implemented the authority provided in such section1599e with respect to probationary periods, including the number, and a demographic summary, of each Department employee removed from the civil service, subject to any disciplinary action (up to and including removal), or who filed a claim or appeal with the Office of Special Counsel or the Equal Employment Opportunity Commission during the second year of any such employee's probationary period.

(c) CONSULTATION.—The analysis and recommendations in the report required under subsection (a) shall be prepared in consultation with Department of Defense employees and managers, labor organizations representing such employees, staff of the Office of Special Counsel and the Equal Employment Opportunity Commission, and attorneys representing Department employees in wrongful termination actions.

SOURCE: Public Law 116–92, 2019.

To carry out the independent review, our RAND study team used a mix of quantitative and qualitative methods, discussed below and in greater detail throughout the report.[9] Our team relied most heavily on statistical analysis of administrative personnel data related to terminations and other disciplinary actions. These data permitted us to directly address the parts of Section 1102 that called for assessments of demographics and distribution patterns and also informed the qualitative analyses.

Statistical Analysis of Administrative Personnel Data

The administrative data we used for our review were provided by the Defense Manpower Data Center (DMDC). We received Appropriated Funds (APF) Civilian Transaction Personnel Files from the DMDC for FY 2015 through FY 2020. We appended to those files select variables from the December 2020 Civilian Transaction Personnel File. The combination provided us with complete transaction records for civilian personnel from November 26, 2015, through December 31, 2020. Personnel actions associated with dates outside October 1, 2015, through December 31, 2020, were dropped. The personnel actions (specifically, different types of appointments) were used to identify covered personnel—those who began a competitive service or SES appointment between November 26, 2015, and December 31, 2018.

The administrative data were used primarily to answer the following questions:

1. What are the demographics of covered personnel in a two-year probationary period during the time frame of interest?
2. What are the demographics of covered personnel subject to termination or other disciplinary actions during the time frame of interest?
3. What patterns are observed among covered personnel terminated or disciplined during their probationary period compared with those not terminated or disciplined?

We used basic statistical techniques, such as calculating means and frequencies, to address the questions pertaining to demographics and relied on regression analyses to identify patterns in terminations and disciplinary actions. For more information on the nature of the administrative data sets and the analytical methods applied to the data, refer to Appendix A. The results of this analysis are described in Chapters Two and Three.

Termination Case Record Analysis

We obtained and analyzed case records for a selection of individuals who were terminated during their probationary periods in accordance with the provisions of 10 U.S.C. 1599e. DCPAS staff used a purposive sampling approach informed, in part, by the results of our statistical analysis to select 48 termination cases for us to review. Specifically, DCPAS first identified cases initiated by supervisors who had experience with multiple probationary period terminations, and then among that subset of cases varied the selection of cases across the military services and the Fourth Estate, then by subagency and occupation. DCPAS requested that the employing agencies of those terminated personnel provide the case files with appropriate redactions to DCPAS so that they could be transmitted to us and subsequently analyzed. Of these 48 cases, files were unable to be located for four cases, and one case file we received did not align with the data, resulting in an analysis sample of 43 cases.

---

[9] The study completed the required human subject protection reviews and was deemed "not human subjects research" by RAND's Institutional Review Board. DoD Defense Human Resources Activity concurred with this determination as a result of its second-level review process.

We began by documenting which cases we received and which we did not and confirming that the case files we received matched on key characteristics to the data (e.g., by confirming that the agency and occupation mentioned in the case files corresponding to a certain scrambled Social Security number aligned with the data for that scrambled social in our DMDC administrative data set). We then catalogued the contents of each case file and developed a semistructured template to capture relevant information we anticipated being able to extract from each case package. We proceeded in an iterative fashion, reviewing a small number of test cases at first, having multiple analysts review the same case, and adjusting the template before expanding to a larger number of cases, repeating the process, and, ultimately, covering the full set of cases. Overall, approximately one in seven cases was reviewed by multiple analysts as a check on consistency.

In addition to the contents of the package, we collected the following elements, when available, from each case file:

- reason for termination
- employee recourse offered or taken
- amount and timing of warning from supervisor to probationer
- any documented positive feedback from supervisor
- whether a performance review was included in the case file
- documentation of leadership review or sign-off on termination
- timeline from appointment to termination (and any documented subsequent actions).

After reviewing the case files, we synthesized the information captured in the template to identify key themes and patterns, both in terms of the structure of the case files (e.g., whether they tend to contain the same materials and degree of documentation) and the substance of the termination cases (e.g., reasons for termination, typical timeline). We paid particular attention to exploring the characteristics of terminations that occurred during the second year, given congressional direction in the FY 2020 NDAA that our review include a discussion of these cases. Findings from our in-depth case analysis are provided in Chapter Four.

Review of OSC and EEO Appeals Data

The FY 2020 NDAA called for demographic information about individuals who filed an appeal with Office of Special Counsel (OSC) or a DoD EEO office for actions taken during their probationary periods. The sensitive nature of appeals data meant that we were not able to access information directly (and, in the case of OSC data, neither was DoD). We relied on DoD to acquire the necessary information from OSC, an external agency, and from the various EEO offices across DoD. To facilitate this effort, we provided DCPAS staff with the scrambled Social Security numbers of personnel in their probationary periods during the time frame of interest based on its analysis of DMDC data, and DMDC unscrambled the Social Security numbers to identify the actual individuals. Equipped with this information, DCPAS then reached out to OSC and to DoD's Office for Diversity, Equity, and Inclusion (ODEI) for assisting in determining how many of those individuals filed an appeal with OSC or one of DoD's EEO offices during their probationary period. ODEI, in turn, tasked 29 agency or component-level EEO offices to provide three numbers: (1) complaints filed during the probationary period; (2) complaints filed during the second year of the probationary period; and (3) complaints filed about being terminated during the probationary period. More detailed demographic information was neither requested nor received.

OSC shared the results of its analysis with DCPAS in July 2021. The 29 DoD EEO offices tasked with providing EEO appeals data varied in the timeliness of their responses, and many of the offices, including those representing the military departments, did not provide any data. As noted earlier in this chapter, the deadline for the draft report was extended to increase the response rate from DoD EEO offices. However, even with a five-month extension, only nine of the 29 offices ultimately provided a response. A breakdown of the responding agencies and a summary of the statistics those EEO offices and OSC provided are included in Chapter Two.

Interviews

We conducted a total of 31 interviews at two points in the study. We used a semistructured interview approach, meaning we had a common set of starting questions for the interviews but also were able to delve into potentially helpful lines of inquiry based on the response to the initial questions or other observations shared by an interview participant. At the outset of the study, we interviewed 12 DoD subject-matter experts in human resources (HR), legal, and EEO. These interviews advanced the study by providing information about how the two-year probationary process had been implemented within DoD and by surfacing issues or concerns of HR and legal professionals, managers and supervisors, and employees. Later in the study, after the statistical analysis was complete, we interviewed representatives from two of the largest unions representing DoD civilian personnel and a representative from an association focused on federal managers and supervisors. Finally, we interviewed seven supervisors and nine HR representatives associated with the termination cases for which we conducted an in-depth qualitative analysis. The later interviews were intended to provide insights on the use and utility of the two-year probationary period, including promising practices, potential misuses, and effects on recruiting, career development, and retention. During the supervisor and HR representative interviews (16 total), we also discussed details about a specific termination case with which they were associated. All the interviews were led by a RAND NDRI study team member. The subject-matter expert interviews and those with union or manager association representatives (15 total) were recorded and transcribed. Given the sensitive nature of the supervisor and HR representative interviews, those interviews were not recorded and transcribed. Instead, a RAND NDRI study team member took detailed notes.

Overall, the interview sample was a purposive one; people were selected by virtue of their positions. This means our results are not generalizable beyond our set of interviewees. They offer insights about how the two-year probationary period is regarded and has been used, but neither the pervasiveness of their views nor the prevalence of practices cited can be determined from the interviews alone.

After all the interviews were complete, two members of our study team analyzed the transcripts and notes using a computer-assisted qualitative data analysis procedure referred to as *coding*. Codes are labels used to organize qualitative data by topic and other characteristics,[10] and coding is a popular approach to analyzing qualitative data that aids data reduction and generation of findings in a way that is transparent and verifiable.[11] We coded the interviews via QSR NVivo, a software package that permits its users to review, categorize, and analyze qualitative data. After researchers assign codes to passages of text, they can later retrieve passages of similarly coded text within and across source documents. We developed a *coding tree*—a set of labels for assigning units of meaning to information compiled during a study, which in turn was the basis for a codebook that we developed to clarify how the codes would be applied.[12] The codebook contained code names, definitions, inclusion and exclusion rules, and examples of interview passages that corresponded to each code.

---

[10] Mathew B. Miles and A. Michael Huberman, *Qualitative Data Analysis: An Expanded Sourcebook*, 2nd ed., Thousand Oaks, Calif.: Sage Publications, 1994.

[11] Phillip Adu, *A Step-by-Step Guide to Qualitative Data Coding*, Oxford: Routledge, 2019.

[12] J. T. DeCuir-Gunby, P. L. Marshall, and A. W. McCulloch, "Developing and Using a Codebook for the Analysis of Interview Data: An Example from a Professional Development Research Project," *Field Methods*, Vol. 23, No. 2, 2011.

We employed a structural coding approach for this study. Codes were based on our study objectives and interview questions and were intended to help us identify themes.[13] After the parent-level coding was completed, the study team worked to draft and apply *child codes*—additional codes intended to parse out parent codes into distinct themes. In both rounds of coding, a single researcher was responsible for applying a code to all the interviews in close coordination with the study lead, which meant no inter-rater reliability checks were needed.

After the coding was complete, we generated coding reports that permitted us to review all the passages tagged with a specific code together. The results of the interviews and subsequent coding are discussed in Chapter Five.

Study Limitations

Although our reliance on multiple data sources strengthened our review, there are important data and analysis shortcomings that readers should bear in mind. First, to assess the effect of a change in the probationary period length, ideally one would compare pre- and post-change outcomes. In this case, that would mean analyzing terminations and disciplinary actions before the two-year probationary period went into effect and comparing them with actions after it went into effect. However, our request for administrative data before 2015 was declined.

The data we did receive also had two notable limitations. We had planned to include performance ratings in our regression models to control for the influence of performance on terminations and disciplinary actions, but we discovered most records were missing performance ratings. In addition, we assumed that all covered personnel had a probationary period length of two years, whereas it is possible some could have had a shorter probationary period because of creditable prior federal service or a longer probationary period from membership in a demonstration project with a three-year probationary period. Customizing probationary period end dates would have been a resource-intensive endeavor beyond the scope of this study. As we discuss later in the report, however, based on our calculations, the number of personnel with a shorter or longer probationary period was relatively small.

A final limitation related to our statistical analysis is that it is not causal. In other words, this means we cannot claim that changing the probationary period length caused more terminations of specific types of personnel—specifically, because we have no way to isolate the effect of the length of the probationary period from the effect of the other variables that are also correlated with our outcomes of interest. Indeed, if DoD had levied this policy randomly to some and not to others across the covered population, then we could have constructed a *treatment group* (newly appointed personnel with a two-year probation) and *control group* (newly appointed personnel with a one-year probation) and we could attribute differences between the two groups in termination or disciplinary actions as the result of the length of the probationary period. In addition, if we had access to pre-2015 data, we could have used that as a natural experiment assess the impact of probationary period length change. However, in light of how the policy was applied and the data available to us, we were limited to a descriptive analysis of what observable factors are correlated with the outcomes of interest.

With respect to the termination case analysis, we had intended to delve into all statistical findings related to organization (e.g., military major command, specific Fourth Estate agency)[14] and occupation that were

---

[13] Johnny Saldaña, *The Coding Manual for Qualitative Researchers*, Thousand Oaks, Calif.: Sage Publications, 2016.

[14] The *Fourth Estate* is a term used to refer to the Office of the Secretary of Defense, defense agencies, and defense field activities outside the three military departments and the unified combatant commands (see Kathleen J. McInnis, *Defense Primer: The Department of Defense*, Washington, D.C.: Congressional Research Service, IF10543, last updated November 8, 2021).

positive and significant (i.e., the characteristics statistically associated with a higher likelihood of termination during the probationary period). Given the way cases were selected, we were unable to take this step, and some occupations with higher termination rates during the probationary period, such as nursing, were not covered in this specific analytic effort.

The notable shortcoming related to the OSC and EEO appeals data is the large amount of missing EEO data. As we will discuss further in the Chapter Two, the organizations with the largest numbers of terminations during probationary periods did not remit appeals data, and the nine organizations that did provide the requested data account for a very small share of terminations. Another concern with these data is they pertain to different groups of personnel; the DoD EEO organizations compiled appeals for all personnel in their probationary period, including personnel with excepted service appointments who are not covered by 10 U.S.C 1599e, while OSC appears to have focused only on covered personnel who were terminated during their probationary periods. Therefore, it is difficult to truly understand the relationship between the results of our statistical analysis, which focused on covered personnel (those with an SES or competitive service appointment), and the occurrence of OSC appeals (e.g., whether there was a large share of appeals filed by a specific type of personnel that our analysis indicated was more likely to be terminated during the probationary period).

Finally, in the process of recruiting interview participants, we encountered soft refusals (i.e., no reply to multiple requests for an interview) and hard refusals (i.e., explicitly declined to participate) from the EEO Commission (EEOC), union representatives, supervisors, and HR representatives. In addition, the Air Force was not represented at all in the supervisor interviews. It is not clear how these nonresponses bias our findings, but as noted earlier, the results of the interviews are not generalizable. Additional research would be needed to understand how prevalent the views shared by interviewees are across DoD overall and to identify differences across types of personnel and between different DoD organizations.

Organization of This Report

The bulk of the report is aligned with the report elements specified in Section 1102 of the FY 2020 NDAA.[15] Chapter Two covers report elements 1 and 6 with a discussion of demographics of those in their probationary periods during the time frame of interest and a summary of OSC and EEO appeals filed by those personnel. Chapter Three reports patterns in removal and disciplinary actions for those in their probationary period, thereby addressing report element 2. Our analysis of termination case records is the focus of Chapter Four and pertains to report element 5. Report elements 3 and 4 are addressed in Chapter Five, our qualitative assessment of areas of concern, promising practices, and the utility of the probationary period. Chapter Six provides recommendations intended to improve how the probationary period is implemented within DoD. Finally, the appendix includes more details about our statistical analysis.

---

[15] Chapters Two through Five start with quoted material from Section 1102 of the FY 2020 NDAA (see Public Law 116–92, 2019).

Demographics

In this chapter, we use DMDC administrative civilian personnel data[1] to describe the personnel newly-appointed to a competitive service or SES position and thus subject to a two-year probationary period during the time frame of interest, November 26, 2015, through December 31, 2018, and the subset of those personnel terminated or disciplined during their probationary period. We also summarize the data pertaining to probationary period appeals that the study sponsor obtained from OSC and DoD EEO offices.

Accordingly, this chapter addresses the following two required report elements:

(1) An assessment and identification of the demographics of each Department of Defense employee who, during such period, was on a probationary period and who was removed from the civil service, subject to any disciplinary action (up to and including removal), or who filed a claim or appeal with the Office of Special Counsel or the Equal Employment Opportunity Commission.

(6) A summary of how the Department has implemented the authority provided in such section 1599e with respect to probationary periods, including the number, and a demographic summary, of each Department employee removed from the civil service, subject to any disciplinary action (up to and including removal), or who filed a claim or appeal with the Office of Special Counsel or the Equal Employment Opportunity Commission during the second year of any such employee's probationary period.

Approach to Identifying the Populations of Interest

To identify the populations of interest for our review, we filtered defense civilian personnel based on appointment types and nature of action (NOA) codes and for the remaining personnel set a probationary period end date.

First, we only kept records associated with competitive service or SES appointments. Following that, we flagged appointments based on NOA codes that provided additional appointment details for those newly appointed to competitive service or SES. This exercise yielded 275 personnel with a new SES appointment and 164,694 personnel with a new competitive service appointment. Given the relatively small number of SES appointments, we opted to combine the personnel with either a new competitive service or SES appointment for a total of 164,969 personnel covered by 10 U.S.C. 1599e.

Our next step was to set a probationary period end date for all personnel. We accomplished this by setting a two-year probation based on first appointment in the time frame of interest. We were aware that actual probationary period lengths could vary, typically being shorter because of creditable federal service or longer

---

[1]   Additional details about this data source and the statistical methods summarized in this chapter are provided in Appendix A.

from inclusion in certain Science and Technology Reinvention Laboratory (STRL) personnel demonstration projects.[2]

Finally, we identified the subsets of these groups that were terminated during their probationary period and/or were subject to disciplinary action. The data file has a specific NOA code for terminations from civil service during a probationary period, which we used for our analysis. We determined that 3,492 competitive service/SES personnel (2.4 percent of all those in their probationary period) were terminated. Turning our attention to disciplinary actions, although supervisors have a wide variety of options available to them in the event of poor employee performance or misconduct, very few of them are recorded consistently in the files we used for our analysis (e.g., the file does not include whether a Performance Improvement Plan was developed or whether a formal reprimand issued). We used in our analysis two measures of suspensions that were included in the DMDC data files, one for suspensions of specific length and one for indefinite suspensions. Using these two measures, we found that 1,304 competitive service/SES personnel (0.8 percent of all those in their probationary period) were subject to disciplinary actions. We also note a small amount of overlap: 14 competitive service/SES personnel were first subject to disciplinary action and then later terminated during their probationary period.

Composition of Personnel in Two-Year Probationary Period

Table 2.1 features a breakdown of personal, occupational, and organizational characteristics for personnel newly appointed to a competitive service or SES position during the time frame of interest. It also provides several statistics related to probationary period terminations: overall terminations, terminations during the first year of the probationary period, terminations during the second year of the probationary period (or later), and the average timing in months for terminations. Finally, Table 2.1 includes information about disciplinary actions. Details on how we used DMDC data for each demographic category are provided in Appendix A. For example, the pay grade at appointment category was created to account for the possibility that new appointees in a junior position may have a different experience during their probationary period than those in a higher pay grade. For all personnel except for those in wage grade (WG) pay plans, the three categories are based on a binning approach developed for a previous study of the DoD civilian workforce.[3] Similarly, given the emphasis on hiring personnel for mission critical occupations (MCOs) and science, technology, engineering, and mathematics (STEM) occupations—and the intense competition for these individuals—we created variables to consider the relationship between being in one of those occupations and the likelihood of termination or disciplinary action during the probationary period.

As shown in the table, covered personnel in their probationary period during the time frame of interest tended to be male, White, non-Hispanic, and in positions covered by bargaining units. Looking at other protected classes beyond gender, race, and ethnicity, 47 percent of those on probation were age 40 or older, 51 percent were veterans, and 18 percent had a disability on record. In addition, the majority of those on probation (59 percent) were in neither MCOs nor STEM occupations. The Navy employed the largest share of those on probation, 33 percent, with the Army relatively close behind. At the subagency level, the U.S. Army Medical Command and the U.S. Air Force Materiel Command employed the largest shares of those on probation at 10 percent and 8 percent, respectively.

---

[2] We focused on STRL demonstration projects because at the time of our study, the Civilian Acquisition Workforce Personnel Demonstration Project, also known as AcqDemo, did not have a longer probationary period for any occupational series.

[3] Christopher Guo, Philip Hall-Partyka, and Susan M. Gates, *Retention and Promotion of High-Quality Civil Service Workers in the Department of Defense Acquisition Workforce*, Santa Monica, Calif.: RAND Corporation, RR-748-OSD, 2014.

Looking at terminations and disciplinary actions, just over 2 percent of covered personnel were terminated during their probationary period. The proportions of those terminated during their first year of probation versus their second year were relatively similar, with more personnel terminated in their first year (52 percent of covered personnel). Few personnel on probation—less than 1 percent—were subject to disciplinary actions in the form of suspensions. This may be because, as we learned in interviews, supervisors are typically encouraged not to engage in progressive discipline, such as Performance Improvement Plans and suspensions for probationary period personnel, but rather to terminate these personnel if less-formal efforts to improve their performance or conduct fail to succeed.

OSC and EEO Appeals Data Analysis

After we identified the populations of interest and produced the summary statistics included in Table 2.1, we then prepared a date file for DCPAS staff to use as part of its requests to OSC and DoD EEO offices for appeals data. The file included the scrambled Social Security numbers of personnel in their probationary or trial period during the time frame of interest and flags to denote whether an individual was terminated and whether he or she had a competitive service/SES appointment or an excepted service appointment. DMDC unscrambled the Social Security numbers to identify the actual individuals, and DCPAS provided a list of names to OSC and ODEI for assisting in determining how many of those individuals filed an appeal with OSC or one of DoD's EEO offices during their probationary period. ODEI, in turn, tasked 29 agency- and component-level servicing EEO Offices to provide three numbers: (1) complaints filed during the probationary period; (2) complaints filed during the second year of the probationary period; and (3) complaints filed about being terminated during the probationary period.

OSC and nine of the 29 agency or component-level EEO offices provided the information requested. Table 2.2 includes a list of the organizations included in the call for appeals data and the numbers they furnished. The OSC data are comprehensive in that they cover all of DoD, but the EEO data fall short in this regard. The nine DoD agencies, all part of the Fourth Estate, that did respond constitute very small percentages of covered personnel and probationary period terminations.[4] Accordingly, these results should be considered low estimates of EEO appeals.

As shown in Table 2.2, during the time frame of interest, 259 probationary period appeals were filed with OSC and 39 with one of the nine DoD EEO offices that submitted data. For OSC, 55 percent of those appeals were filed during the second year of the probationary period. For the eight DoD EEO offices that reported appeals filed during the second year, 44 percent of appeals were filed during that window. Finally, 20 percent of OSC appeals and 64 percent of DoD EEO appeals (for nine DoD subagencies) filed during the probationary period were about being terminated. All in all, the number of appeals is a small number relative to the number of covered personnel overall and to those terminated, but the large amount of missing data means this is not a definitive finding. Additional research is warranted to understand the number and nature of EEO-related appeals filed by those in their probationary periods, particularly those terminated during that period.

---

[4]   The DMDC data files we used for our analysis do not include separate values for Defense Counterintelligence and Security Agency and National Geospatial-Intelligence Agency. This means we were unable to calculate either the number of covered personnel or the number of probationary period terminations associated with the nine sub-agencies whose EEO offices submitted appeals data. Looking at the seven subagencies included in the DMDC data files, together they include 2,350 covered personnel (less than 1 percent of all covered personnel) and 40 terminations (less than 1 percent of probationary period terminations during the time frame of interest). The entire Fourth Estate includes 26,284 (16 percent) of covered personnel and 729 (21 percent) of probationary period terminations.

TABLE 2.1
Characteristics of Personnel Newly Appointed to Competitive Service/SES Positions (November 26, 2015–December 31, 2018)

Demographic Category	Characteristic	Covered Personnel (n=164,969)	All Terminations (n=3,492)	First-Year Terminations (n=1,805)	Second-Year Terminations (n=1,687)	Average Termination Timing (months)	All Disciplined (n=1,304)
Age	Age 40 or younger	47.7%	42.2%	42.4%	41.9%	12.40	49.7%
	Older than 40	52.3%	57.8%	57.6%	58.1%	12.43	50.3%
Gender	Female	35.6%	33.8%	34.6%	33.1%	12.43	20.7%
	Male	64.4%	66.2%	65.4%	66.9%	12.42	79.3%
Race	White	71.3%	63.0%	62.0%	64.0%	12.56	67.3%
	Black	15.3%	23.7%	25.0%	22.2%	11.98	19.0%
	Asian	5.6%	4.2%	3.4%	5.1%	13.23	4.4%
	American Indian or Alaska Native	1.2%	2.0%	1.9%	2.1%	12.76	1.6%
	Hawaiian/Pacific Islander	1.0%	0.9%	0.8%	0.9%	12.86	0.8%
	Other race	3.7%	4.5%	5.2%	3.9%	11.77	3.9%
	Unknown	2.0%	1.7%	1.8%	1.7%	12.45	2.9%
Hispanic	Yes	6.9%	6.2%	6.1%	6.3%	12.41	6.6%
	No	93.1%	93.8%	93.9%	93.7%	12.42	93.4%
Veteran	Yes	50.7%	45.1%	46.8%	43.3%	11.99	57.1%
	No	49.3%	54.9%	53.2%	56.7%	12.78	42.9%
Disability status	Yes	18.4%	21.7%	22.9%	20.4%	11.70	18.7%
	No	81.6%	78.3%	77.1%	79.6%	12.62	81.3%

Table 2.1—Continued

Demographic Category	Characteristic	Covered Personnel (n=164,969)	All Terminations (n=3,492)	First-Year Terminations (n=1,805)	Second-Year Terminations (n=1,687)	Average Termination Timing (months)	All Disciplined (n=1,304)
Education level	No college	37.8%	53.7%	58.4%	48.5%	11.67	55.3%
	Some college	16.4%	16.9%	15.1%	18.8%	13.07	22.0%
	Bachelor's degree or higher	45.8%	29.4%	26.4%	32.7%	13.42	22.7%
Pay grade at appointment	Entry-level	41.4%	57.0%	60.6%	53.3%	11.81	40.3%
	Mid-level	50.5%	36.6%	34.0%	39.4%	13.10	50.6%
	Senior-level	4.8%	2.1%	1.7%	2.4%	13.86	3.4%
	SES	0.2%	N/A	N/A	N/A	N/A	N/A
In bargaining unit	Yes	65.1%	78.7%	80.5%	76.7%	12.15	75.5%
	No	34.9%	21.3%	19.5%	23.3%	13.42	24.5%
Supervisory status	Yes	6.0%	3.0%	2.5%	3.6%	13.57	5.8%
	No	94.0%	97.0%	97.5%	96.4%	12.38	94.2%
Locality Pay Area (LPA)	Washington, D.C.	9.2%	6.9%	6.6%	7.2%	12.86	6.4%
	Seattle/Tacoma	3.6%	6.2%	6.6%	5.7%	11.49	3.3%
	San Diego	2.9%	3.7%	3.7%	3.7%	12.51	2.4%
	Los Angeles	2.5%	1.7%	1.8%	1.5%	11.83	1.5%
	Boston	1.9%	2.5%	2.7%	2.4%	11.05	3.4%
	Hawaii	2.4%	1.9%	1.3%	2.6%	14.98	1.7%
	All other LPAs (including rest of United States)	77.7%	77.1%	77.3%	76.8%	12.45	81.4%

Table 2.1—Continued

Demographic Category	Characteristic	Covered Personnel (n=164,969)	All Terminations (n=3,492)	First-Year Terminations (n=1,805)	Second-Year Terminations (n=1,687)	Average Termination Timing (months)	All Disciplined (n=1,304)
Service/component							
	Air Force	20.2%	13.9%	12.5%	15.4%	13.25	20.7%
	Army	30.9%	31.0%	31.1%	31.0%	12.39	28.4%
	Navy	32.8%	34.2%	32.7%	35.7%	12.71	37.6%
	Fourth Estate	15.9%	20.9%	23.7%	17.9%	11.45	13.0%
Subagency							
Air Force	Air Combat Cmd	1.3%	1.1%	1.3%	0.8%	10.41	0.8%
	Air Educ and Training Cmd	2.1%	1.4%	1.5%	1.4%	12.55	1.8%
	Air National Guard Units (Title 32)	0.3%	N/A	N/A	N/A	N/A	N/A
	Headquarters, USAF Reserve Cmd	2.2%	0.9%	0.7%	1.1%	14.23	1.5%
	USAF Civilian Career Training	1.1%	0.5%	N/A	0.7%	15.77	N/A
	USAF Materiel Cmd	8.1%	7.8%	6.8%	8.9%	13.54	13.0%
Army	Army National Guard Units (Title 32)	0.7%	N/A	N/A	N/A	N/A	N/A
	Field Operating Offices, Office of the Secretary of the Army	0.4%	N/A	N/A	N/A	N/A	N/A
	U.S. Army Corps of Engineers	3.6%	3.7%	3.6%	3.7%	12.88	3.2%
	U.S. Army Installation Mgmt Cmd	3.5%	3.7%	4.0%	3.4%	11.48	4.7%
	U.S. Army Medical Cmd	10.2%	13.7%	12.6%	14.9%	12.93	7.2%
	U.S. Army Reserve Cmd	1.9%	2.5%	3.0%	2.0%	10.69	3.1%

Table 2.1—Continued

Demographic Category	Characteristic	Covered Personnel (n=164,969)	All Terminations (n=3,492)	First-Year Terminations (n=1,805)	Second-Year Terminations (n=1,687)	Average Termination Timing (months)	All Disciplined (n=1,304)
Navy	Naval Air Systems Cmd	5.3%	4.7%	3.9%	5.6%	13.75	5.0%
	Naval Educ and Training Cmd	1.2%	0.8%	0.7%	0.9%	13.31	1.2%
	Naval Facilities Engineering Cmd	2.4%	2.6%	2.1%	3.1%	14.11	1.8%
	Naval Medical Cmd	2.4%	4.0%	4.5%	3.4%	11.09	2.2%
	Naval Sea Systems Cmd	5.4%	1.8%	1.7%	1.8%	12.35	2.9%
	Navy Install Cmd	1.9%	2.7%	2.7%	2.8%	11.60	2.5%
	Space and Naval Warfare Systems Cmd	1.2%	0.5%	N/A	0.6%	16.63	N/A
	U.S. Fleet Forces Cmd	4.3%	6.7%	6.5%	6.9%	13.02	11.7%
	Marine Corps	2.0%	2.1%	1.9%	2.3%	12.44	1.8%
	U.S. Pacific Fleet	3.4%	6.4%	6.5%	6.3%	12.12	5.2%
Fourth Estate	Defense Commissary Agency	4.0%	8.6%	12.7%	4.2%	8.92	2.5%
	Defense Contract Mgmt Agency	1.9%	1.0%	0.9%	1.0%	13.59	N/A
	Defense Finance and Accounting Svc	2.2%	2.6%	2.0%	3.3%	14.21	1.2%
	Defense Logistics Agency	3.7%	5.4%	4.5%	6.3%	13.20	5.5%
	DoD Education Activity	0.2%	0.3%	0.6%	N/A	10.11	N/A
All other subagencies (DoD-wide)	All other	22.9%	14.2%	14.3%	14.2%	12.61	18.6%

15

Table 2.1—Continued

Demographic Category	Characteristic	Covered Personnel (*n*=164,969)	All Terminations (*n*=3,492)	First-Year Terminations (*n*=1,805)	Second-Year Terminations (*n*=1,687)	Average Termination Timing (months)	All Disciplined (*n*=1,304)
MCO							
	MCO/STEM	14.1%	10.3%	9.9%	10.8%	12.87	6.3%
	MCO/non-STEM	14.8%	9.0%	7.4%	10.7%	13.39	11.8%
	Non-MCO/STEM	12.0%	6.1%	5.5%	6.8%	13.51	4.4%

SOURCE: Authors' analysis of DMDC data.

NOTES: Table provides number of personnel newly appointed from November 26, 2015, through December 31, 2018. N/A = ten or fewer personnel fit this category; precise number not provided to protect personnel's confidentiality. MCOs are based on FY 2015 and FY 2020 MCO lists provided by DoD sponsor and STEM occupations based on 2012 DoD STEM Occupation Taxonomy. Admin = Administration; Cmd = Command; Educ = Education; Eng = Engineering; IT = Information Technology; Mgmt = Management; Svcs = Services; USAF = U.S. Air Force.

TABLE 2.2

OSC and EEO Appeals Filed by Newly Appointed Personnel (November 26, 2015– December 31, 2018)

Organization	All Appeals Filed During the Probationary Period	Appeals Filed During the Second Year of the Probationary Period	All Appeals Filed About Being Terminated During the Probationary Period
Office of Special Counsel	259	143	52
DoD EEO Offices That Reported Appeals Data:	39	11	25
Defense Advanced Research Projects Agency, Defense Contract Audit Agency, Defense Counterintelligence and Security Agency, Defense Human Resources Activity, Defense Media Activity, Defense Security Cooperation Agency, Department of Defense Education Activity, Missile Defense Agency, and National Geospatial-Intelligence Agency			

SOURCE: Data provided by DCPAS.

NOTES: Organizations that did not respond to the data request include the following: Army & Air Force Exchange Service, Defense Commissary Agency, Defense Finance and Accounting Service, Defense Health Agency, Defense Intelligence Agency, Defense Logistics Agency, Defense Technical Information Center, Defense Threat Reduction Agency, Defense Contract Management Agency, Defense Information Systems Agency, Joint Staff, National Guard Bureau, National Reconnaissance Office, National Security Agency, Office of Inspector General, Air Force, Army, Navy, Uniformed Services University of the Health Sciences, and Washington Headquarters Service. OSC reported using a file of 169,976 personnel for its inquiry. DoD EEO offices used a file with 206,657 records. We surmise that the difference may be that OSC focused only on covered personnel in its research, while DoD EEO offices also included personnel with excepted service appointments.

CHAPTER THREE

Patterns in Removals and Disciplinary Action

In this chapter, we report the results of our statistical analysis of DMDC administrative civilian personnel data. Specifically, we identified what personnel characteristics were related to the probability of (1) termination during the probationary period, (2) disciplinary action during the probationary period, or (3) probationary period terminations after the first year of probation after controlling for other observable characteristics available in the data files. Our focus was on covered personnel appointed during the time frame of interest, November 26, 2015, through December 31, 2018, but we also analyzed terminations and disciplinary actions for personnel newly appointed to excepted service positions to provide a comparison group.

Accordingly, this chapter addresses the following required report element:

> (2) A statistical assessment of the distribution patterns with respect to any removal from the civil service during such period of, or any disciplinary action (up to and including a removal) taken during such period against, any Department employee while the employee was on a probationary period.

Approach

To identify patterns related to terminations and disciplinary actions, we used regression analysis. Here we provide a high-level discussion of our analytic approach. A detailed description of our statistical methodology is available in Appendix A.

In the regression models, we control for (i.e., take into account) the personnel characteristics summarized in Chapter Two. Given the potential influence of occupation in termination and disciplinary actions decisions (e.g., supervisors may be less inclined to remove someone in a hard-to-fill MCO), we examined occupations in several ways. First, we considered four groups of occupations based on DoD's designations of certain occupations as MCO and/or STEM: MCO/STEM, MCO/non-STEM, non-MCO/STEM, and non-MCO/non-STEM. To ensure we were not losing an important level of detail through our use of occupation groups, we then ran a series of models in which one of the four MCO/STEM groups was disaggregated (i.e., each occupation was included in the model as a distinct variable). We found that there was enough variation across specific MCO/non-STEM occupations to warrant presenting their marginal effects separately. Accordingly, in our second model, we retained three of the occupation groups—MCO/STEM, non-MCO/STEM, and non-MCO/non-STEM—and included as separate variables all the specific occupations that constitute the MCO/non-STEM group. For our third model, we included as separate variables the occupations with at least 1 percent of the covered personnel.[1] Table 3.1 lists the variables in each model and specifies each referent group. Referent groups are necessary because all of the explanatory variables in our models are categorical. This means that our results are expressed as differences from the referent group. For variables that pertain to protected classes (e.g., gender, race, ethnicity, age, veteran status, and disability status), the referent group is the nonprotected class. For other variables, typically we used a smaller group as the referent. In each

---

[1]   Lists of the occupations included in each group are available in Appendix A.

TABLE 3.1

Regression Model Summary

Characteristic	Model 1	Model 2	Model 3
Age 40 or older (referent group: younger than age 40)	X	X	X
Gender (referent group: male)	X	X	X
Race (referent group: White)			
Black	X	X	X
Asian	X	X	X
American Indian or Alaska Native	X	X	X
Hawaiian/Pacific Islander	X	X	X
Other race	X	X	X
Hispanic ethnicity (referent group: not Hispanic)	X	X	X
Veteran (referent group: non-veteran)	X	X	X
Disability status (referent group: no known disability)	X	X	X
Education level (referent group: no college)			
Some college	X	X	X
Bachelor's degree or more	X	X	X
Pay grade at appointment (referent group: entry-level)			
Mid-level	X	X	X
Senior-level	X	X	X
SES level	X	X	X
In bargaining unit (referent group: not in a bargaining unit)	X	X	X
Supervisor (referent group: not a supervisor)	X	X	X
LPA (referent group: all other LPAs [including the rest of the United States])			
Washington, D.C.	X	X	X
Seattle/Tacoma	X	X	X
San Diego	X	X	X
Los Angeles	X	X	X
Boston	X	X	X
Hawaii	X	X	X
Service/component (referent group: Fourth Estate)			
Air Force	X	X	X
Army	X	X	X
Navy	X	X	X

Table 3.1—Continued

Characteristic	Model 1	Model 2	Model 3
Subagency (referent group: all other subagencies)			
Air Force	X	X	X
Air Combat Cmd	X	X	X
Air Educ and Training Cmd	X	X	X
Air National Guard Units (Title 32)	X	X	X
Headquarters, USAF Reserve Cmd	X	X	X
USAF Civilian Career Training	X	X	X
USAF Materiel Cmd	X	X	X
Army			
Army National Guard Units (Title 32)	X	X	X
Field Operating Offices, Office of the Secretary of the Army	X	X	X
U.S. Army Corps of Engineers	X	X	X
U.S. Army Installation Mgmt Cmd	X	X	X
U.S. Army Medical Cmd	X	X	X
U.S. Army Reserve Cmd	X	X	X
Navy			
Naval Air Systems Cmd	X	X	X
Naval Educ and Training Cmd	X	X	X
Naval Facilities Engineering Cmd	X	X	X
Naval Medical Cmd	X	X	X
Naval Sea Systems Cmd	X	X	X
Navy Installations Cmd	X	X	X
Space and Naval Warfare Sys Cmd	X	X	X
U.S. Fleet Forces Cmd	X	X	X
Marine Corps	X	X	X
U.S. Pacific Fleet	X	X	X
Fourth Estate			
Defense Commissary Agency	X	X	X
Defense Contract Mgmt Agency	X	X	X
Defense Finance and Accounting Svcs	X	X	X
Defense Logistics Agency	X	X	X
DoD Education Activity	X	X	X

Table 3.1—Continued

Characteristic	Model 1	Model 2	Model 3
MCOs (referent group: non-MCO/non-STEM)			
MCO/STEM	X	X	
MCO/non-STEM	X		
Non-MCO/STEM	X	X	
MCO non-STEM occupations (referent group: non-MCO/non-STEM)			
Accounting		X	
Administrative Officer		X	
Auditing		X	
Budget Analysis		X	
Contracting		X	
Criminal Investigating		X	
Educ and Training Technician		X	
Educ and Vocational Training		X	
Explosives Safety		X	
Financial Admin and Program		X	
Fire Protection and Prevention		X	
General Educ and Training		X	
General Supply		X	
HR Mgmt		X	
Inventory Mgmt		X	
Language Specialist		X	
Physical Therapist		X	
Police		X	
Production Control		X	
Public Affairs		X	
Quality Assurance		X	
Safety and Occ Health Mgmt		X	
Security Admin		X	
Social Work		X	
Telecommunications		X	
Traffic Mgmt		X	
Training Instruction		X	
Transportation Specialist		X	

Table 3.1—Continued

Characteristic	Model 1	Model 2	Model 3
Occupations with at least 1% of the covered workforce			
Professional			
Contracting			X
Economist			X
Mechanical Eng			X
Administrative			
Financial Admin and Program			X
HR Mgmt			X
IT Mgmt			X
Logistics Mgmt			X
Mgmt and Program Analysis			X
Misc Admin and Program			X
Security Admin			X
Technical			X
General Business and Industry			X
Sports Specialist			X
Clerical			
HR Assistance			X
Misc Clerk and Assistant			X
Sales Store Clerical			
Other White Collar			X
Nurse			X
Police			X
Security Guard			
Blue Collar			
Aircraft Mechanic			X
Misc Warehousing and Stock Handling			X
Unnamed Occupations			
1.institutionaladmin			X
1.blankocc2			X
1.positionclassification			

SOURCE: Authors' analysis of DMDC data.

NOTES: We were unable to identify three occupations, which we refer to as *Unnamed Occupations*, that had at least 1 percent of covered personnel, but we included them in Model 3 for completeness. Admin = Administration; Cmd = Command; Educ = Education; Eng = Engineering; IT = Information Technology; Mgmt = Management; Svcs = Services; USAF = U.S. Air Force.

case, the referent group is a decision we made that can be changed. However, when we shared preliminary results with the sponsor in a project update, the sponsor was satisfied with our choice of referent groups and the implications that had for interpreting the results.

As a reminder, the results of our regression analysis are not causal, meaning that we cannot conclude that changing the probationary period length caused certain personnel to be terminated more or less frequently. Instead, the results mean that after taking observable factors into account, certain characteristics are correlated with being terminated or disciplined during one's probationary period.

Results

In the sections that follow, we share findings about the probability of (1) termination during the probationary period, (2) disciplinary action during the probationary period, and (3) termination after the first year of probation, conditional on being terminated, after controlling for other characteristics. In each section, we review the statistically significant findings in Model 1, which we regard as our main model. For occupational measures, which varied across the models, we report the results of all three models. We also note instances, if any, in which Models 2 and 3 yielded statistically significant results different from Model 1 for characteristics other than occupation. Finally, we consider the intersection of statistically significant results across different outcomes, or in other words, when the same characteristic is related to both the probability of termination during the probationary period and the probability of disciplinary action or when the same characteristic is related to both the probability of termination during the probationary period at all and to the probability of being terminated after the first year of probation.

Characteristics Related to the Probability of Termination During the Probationary Period

The results of our analysis of probationary period termination patterns are provided in Tables 3.2 and 3.3. Table 3.2 features all the results of Model 1 except for occupation characteristics, and Table 3.3 includes occupation-related results from all three models. In each table, the first column lists the characteristics included in the model and identifies the referent group for each category. The referent group was omitted from the analysis and is the basis for comparison for other attributes within a specific category, such as race. The second column shows whether a characteristic was statistically significant,[2] meaning that even when other observable factors are considered, that characteristic has a significant relationship with the outcome of interest—in this case, the probability of a probationary period termination. The third column shows the direction of the effect in relation to the referent group. For example, in Table 3.2 our analysis indicated that age was a significant factor in explaining termination patterns and the direction of the effect was negative (i.e., lower or decreased probability). Specifically, covered personnel ages 40 or older were less likely to be terminated during probation compared with covered personnel younger than age 40. The final column, magnitude of effect, provides some information about how strong the relationship was. We used a threshold of 0.10 percentage points in this summary; the full list of coefficients providing magnitude is available in Appendix A. This means, for example, if on average those age 40 or older face a 2.1 percent chance of being terminated, then those younger than age 40 face a 2.0 percent chance of being terminated. Effects less than 0.10 percentage points are still both statistically significant and notable, especially when considered in combination with other characteristics; for ease of presentation, here we focus on the strongest relationships.

---

[2] We used a threshold of p-value < .05 for statistical significance.

TABLE 3.2

Regression Analysis Summary: Characteristics Related to the Probability of Termination During the Probationary Period, Model 1

Variable	Statistically Significant	Direction of Effect	Magnitude of at Least 0.10 Percentage Points
Age 40 or older (referent group: younger than age 40)			
Age 40 and older	Yes	Negative	
Gender (referent group: male)			
Female	Yes	Negative	
Missing			
Race (referent group: White)			
Black	Yes	Positive	Yes
Asian	Yes	Negative	
American Indian or Alaska Native	Yes	Positive	Yes
Hawaiian/Pacific Islander			
Other	Yes	Positive	
Missing			
Hispanic ethnicity (referent group: not Hispanic)			
Hispanic	Yes	Negative	
Missing			
Veteran (referent group: non-veteran)			
Yes	Yes	Negative	
Missing			
Disability status (referent group: no known disability)			
Yes	Yes	Positive	
Unknown			
Education level (referent group: no college)			
Some college	Yes	Negative	
Bachelor's degree or higher	Yes	Negative	
Missing			
Pay grade at appointment (referent group: entry-level)			
Mid-level	Yes	Negative	
Senior-level	Yes	Negative	Yes
SES level			
Missing			
In bargaining unit (referent group: not in a bargaining unit)			
In bargaining unit	Yes	Positive	
Missing			

Table 3.2—Continued

Variable	Statistically Significant	Direction of Effect	Magnitude of at Least 0.10 Percentage Points
Supervisor (referent group: not a supervisor)			
Yes			
Missing			
LPA (referent group: all other LPAs [including the rest of the United States])			
Washington, D.C.			
Seattle/Tacoma			
San Diego			
Los Angeles			
Boston			
Hawaii	Yes	Negative	Yes
Not in an LPA			
Missing LPA			
Service/component (referent group: Fourth Estate)			
Air Force	Yes	Negative	Yes
Army	Yes	Negative	
Navy	Yes	Negative	
Missing			
Subagency (referent group: all other subagencies)			
Air Force			
Air Combat Cmd	Yes	Positive	
Air Educ and Training Cmd			
Air National Guard Units (Title 32)			
Headquarters, USAF Reserve Cmd			
USAF Civilian Career Training			
USAF Materiel Cmd	Yes	Positive	
Army			
Army National Guard Units (Title 32)	Yes	Negative	Yes
Field Operating Offices, Office of the Secretary of the Army			
U.S. Army Corps of Engineers	Yes	Positive	
U.S. Army Installation Mgmt Cmd			
U.S. Army Medical Cmd	Yes	Positive	Yes
U.S. Army Reserve Cmd	Yes	Positive	Yes

Table 3.2—Continued

Variable	Statistically Significant	Direction of Effect	Magnitude of at Least 0.10 Percentage Points
Navy			
Naval Air Systems Cmd	Yes	Positive	
Naval Educ and Training Cmd			
Naval Facilities Engineering Cmd	Yes	Positive	Yes
Naval Medical Cmd	Yes	Positive	Yes
Naval Sea Systems Cmd			
Navy Installations Cmd	Yes	Positive	Yes
Space and Naval Warfare Sys Cmd			
U.S. Fleet Forces Cmd	Yes	Positive	Yes
Marine Corps	Yes	Positive	Yes
U.S. Pacific Fleet	Yes	Positive	Yes
Fourth Estate			
Defense Commissary Agency	Yes	Positive	
Defense Contract Mgmt Agency	Yes	Negative	
Defense Finance and Accounting Svcs			
Defense Logistics Agency			
DoD Education Activity	Yes	Positive	Yes

SOURCE: Authors' analysis of DMDC data.

NOTES: Number of observations for covered personnel = 164,345. Statistically significant results are significant at p-value < .05. Admin = Administration; Cmd = Command; Educ = Education; Eng = Engineering; IT = Information Technology; Mgmt = Management; Svcs = Services; USAF = U.S. Air Force.

TABLE 3.3

Regression Analysis Summary: Occupational Characteristics Related to the Probability of Termination During the Probationary Period, All Models

Variable	Statistically Significant	Direction of Effect	Magnitude of at Least 0.10 Percentage Points
Model 1			
MCO/STEM	Yes	Negative	
MCO/non-STEM	Yes	Negative	
Non-MCO/STEM	Yes	Negative	
Model 2			
Occupation group			
MCO/STEM	Yes	Negative	
Non-MCO/STEM	Yes	Negative	

Table 3.3—Continued

Variable	Statistically Significant	Direction of Effect	Magnitude of at Least 0.10 Percentage Points
MCO/non-STEM occupations			
Accounting	Yes	Positive	
Administrative Officer			
Auditing			
Budget Analysis			
Contracting	Yes	Negative	
Criminal Investigating			
Educ and Training Technician	Yes	Negative	
Educ and Vocational Training			
Explosives Safety			
Financial Admin and Program	Yes	Negative	
Fire Protection and Prevention	Yes	Negative	
General Educ and Training			
General Supply			
HR Mgmt	Yes	Negative	
Inventory Mgmt			
Language Specialist			
Physical Therapist			
Police			
Production Control			
Public Affairs			
Quality Assurance			
Safety and Occ Health Mgmt			
Security Admin	Yes	Negative	
Social Work			
Telecommunications			
Traffic Mgmt			
Training Instruction			
Transportation Specialist			

Table 3.3—Continued

Variable	Statistically Significant	Direction of Effect	Magnitude of at Least 0.10 Percentage Points
Model 3			
Professional			
Contracting	Yes	Negative	
Economist	Yes	Negative	
Mechanical Eng	Yes	Negative	
Administrative			
Financial Admin and Program	Yes	Negative	
HR Mgmt	Yes	Negative	
IT Mgmt			
Logistics Mgmt	Yes	Negative	
Mgmt and Program Analysis			
Misc Admin and Program			
Security Admin	Yes	Negative	
Technical			
General Business and Industry	Yes	Negative	
Sports Specialist			
Clerical			
HR Assistance			
Misc Clerk and Assistant	Yes	Negative	
Sales Store Clerical			
Other White Collar			
Nurse	Yes	Positive	
Police			
Security Guard			
Blue Collar			
Aircraft Mechanic			
Misc Warehousing and Stock Handling	Yes	Positive	
Unnamed Occupations			
1.institutionaladmin			
1.blankocc2	Yes	Negative	
1.positionclassification			

SOURCE: Authors' analysis of DMDC data.

NOTES: Number of observations for covered personnel: Model 1 = 164,345, Model 2 = 164,161, and Model 3 = 164,345. Statistically significant results are significant at p-value < .05. Admin = Administration; Cmd = Command; Educ = Education; Eng = Engineering; IT = Information Technology; Mgmt = Management; Svcs = Services; USAF = U.S. Air Force.

We found that many characteristics were significantly related to the probability of probationary period terminations, including several protected classes, as follows:

- factors related to a higher probability of termination:
  - **personal attributes**, including being Black, American Indian or Alaska Native, or Other race; having a disability; or being in a position covered by a bargaining unit
  - **organizational characteristics**, including working at specific subagencies within the Air Force, Army, Navy, and the Fourth Estate
  - **occupations**, specifically, the Accounting, Nurse, and Miscellaneous Warehousing and Stock Handling occupations.
- factors related to a lower probability of termination:
  - **personal attributes**, including being age 40 or older; female; Asian; Hispanic; a veteran; having some college education or a bachelor's degree; or being in a mid-level or senior-level pay grade at the time of appointment
  - **organizational characteristics**, including being in the Hawaii LPA; working in one of the military services (compared with the Fourth Estate); working at Army National Guard Units (Title 32) or Defense Contract Management Agency
  - **occupations**, include MCO/STEM, MCO/non-STEM, and non-MCO/STEM occupations in general and several specific occupations: Contracting, Education and Training Technician, Financial Administration and Program, Fire Protection and Prevention, HR Management, Security Administration, Economist, Mechanical Engineering, Logistics Management, General Business and Industry, and Miscellaneous Clerk and Assistant.

Based on percentage point difference, a subset of those factors had a comparatively large association with the probability of probationary period termination. Specifically, Black personnel, American Indian or Alaska Native personnel, and those working in one of nine subagencies (including both Army and Naval Medical Commands) had a relatively *high* probability of termination compared with other probationary employees. Conversely, those in a senior-level pay grade at the time of appointment, those working in the Hawaii LPA, Air Force personnel, and those working in Army National Guard Units (Title 32) had a relatively *low* probability of termination compared other probationary employees.

Looking across our different model specifications, in which we used different sets of variables for occupations, the results are substantively the same with a few notable differences. Specifically, being older (age 40 and older) and being in the Army are not statistically significant characteristics across all models. In addition, being in the Naval Sea Systems Command was not statistically significant in our main model. However, in one other model specification (Model 3, which includes the occupations with at least 1 percent of covered personnel), being in this command compared with all other subagencies is associated with a significantly lower probability of probationary period termination. There were also some instances in which a characteristic was statistically significant in all three models, but the magnitude of the effect varied. All the magnitude values are available for review in Appendix A.

Thinking about how to interpret these findings, working in many of the subagencies included in our model was significantly associated with a higher probability of probationary period termination. This may be because these organizations had a relatively large share of new hires with poor performance or misconduct, or it could be because these organizations are well-acquainted with using the probationary period as the final stage in the hiring process. Looking at factors significantly associated with a lower rate of probationary period termination, it is possible that more highly educated and more senior hires (based on pay grade at entry) went through a more extensive, resource-intensive hiring process than other personnel to ensure they were a good fit and thus less likely to warrant termination. In addition, working in a STEM occupation, both

MCO and non-MCO ones, was also significantly associated with a lower probability of probationary period termination. This may be because STEM personnel are in high demand, difficult to recruit, and as a result, supervisors are less inclined to terminate them.

Characteristics Related to the Probability of Disciplinary Action During the Probationary Period

Tables 3.4 and 3.5 summarize the results of our analysis of probationary period disciplinary action patterns. As a reminder, our measure of disciplinary actions is based on suspensions; disciplinary actions, such as reprimands, were not in the data set we used. The structure of the tables is the same as that for Tables 3.2 and 3.3, except variables without significant results were omitted for ease of presentation. Overall, there were fewer statistically significant findings related to probationary period disciplinary actions. This may be due, in part, to the relatively low number of disciplinary actions observed—1,304 covered personnel were suspended during their probationary period. Once again, there were findings related to a protected class: Compared with White personnel, Black personnel had a higher probability of being terminated during their probationary period. Other characteristics that were significantly related to the probability of probationary period disciplinary action include the following:

- factors related to a higher probability of disciplinary action:
  - **personal attributes**, including being in a position covered by a bargaining unit and being a supervisor
  - **organizational characteristics**, including working in the Boston LPA and working at specific sub-agencies in the Air Force, Army, and Navy
  - **occupations**, specifically HR Management and Inventory Management.
- factors related to a lower probability of disciplinary action:
  - **personal attributes**, including being female and having a bachelor's degree or higher
  - **organizational characteristics**, specifically working in the Defense Commissary Agency or Defense Contract Management Agency
  - **occupations**, including MCO/STEM and non-MCO/STEM occupations in general and the Economist, Mechanical Engineering, IT Management, or Miscellaneous Clerk and Assistant occupations in particular.[3]

Based on percentage point difference, if we use the same 0.10 percentage points threshold as before, only a missing value variable (for service/component) falls into this category. A look at effect sizes under the 0.10 percentage points mark (see Appendix A) reveals that the largest effects are 0.07 percentage points for U.S. Fleet Forces Command and Defense Contract Management Agency.

Looking at different model specifications, the results are substantively the same with a few instances in which characteristics not significant in our main model were significant in another model. Specifically, in Model 2 (with MCO/non-STEM occupations all included as separate variables versus grouped into a single variable), being American Indian or Alaska Native and being a veteran were both associated with a higher probability of probationary period disciplinary action compared with being White or being a non-veteran, respectively. In both Models 2 and 3 (Model 3 includes the occupations with at least 1 percent of covered personnel), working in Naval Education and Training Command was associated with a higher probability of probationary period disciplinary action compared with all other subagencies. There were also some instances

---

[3] Two of the unnamed occupations were also associated with a lower probability of disciplinary action during probation.

TABLE 3.4

Regression Analysis Summary: Characteristics Related to the Probability of Disciplinary Action During the Probationary Period, Model 1

Variable	Direction of Effect	Magnitude of at Least 0.10 Percentage Points
Gender (referent group: male)		
Female	Negative	
Race (referent group: White)		
Black	Positive	
Missing	Positive	
Education level (referent group: no college)		
Bachelor's degree or higher	Negative	
In bargaining unit (referent group: not in a bargaining unit)		
In bargaining unit	Positive	
Supervisor (referent group: not a supervisor)		
Yes	Positive	
LPA (referent group: all other LPAs [including the rest of the United States])		
Boston	Positive	
Missing LPA	Positive	
Service/component (referent group: Fourth Estate)		
Missing	Positive	
Subagency (referent group: all other subagencies)		
Air Force		
Air Force Materiel Cmd	Positive	
Army		
U.S. Army Reserve Cmd	Positive	
Navy		
U.S. Fleet Forces Cmd	Positive	
U.S. Pacific Fleet	Positive	
Fourth Estate		
Defense Commissary Agency	Negative	
Defense Contract Mgmt Agency	Negative	

SOURCE: Authors' analysis of DMDC data.

NOTES: Number of observations for covered personnel = 164,827. Statistically significant results are significant at p-value < .05. Table only includes statistically significant results. Refer to Table 3.2 for full list of variables included in the model. Admin = Administration; Cmd = Command; Educ = Education; Eng = Engineering; IT = Information Technology; Mgmt = Management; Svcs = Services; USAF = U.S. Air Force.

TABLE 3.5

Regression Analysis Summary: Occupational Characteristics Related to the Probability of Disciplinary Action During the Probationary Period, All Models

Variable	Direction of Effect	Magnitude of at Least 0.10 Percentage Points
Model 1		
MCO/STEM	Negative	
Non-MCO/STEM	Negative	
Model 2: Occupation group		
MCO/STEM	Negative	
Non-MCO/STEM	Negative	
MCO/non-STEM occupations		
HR Mgmt	Positive	
Inventory Mgmt	Positive	
Model 3		
Professional		
Economist	Negative	
Mechanical Eng	Negative	
Administrative		
HR Mgmt	Positive	
IT Mgmt	Negative	
Clerical		
Misc Clerk and Assistant	Negative	
Unnamed Occupations		
1.blankocc2	Negative	
1.positionclassification	Negative	

SOURCE: Authors' analysis of DMDC data.

NOTES: Number of observations for covered personnel: Model 1 = 164,827, Model 2 = 163,344, and Model 3 = 164,827. Statistically significant results are significant at p-value < .05. Table only includes statistically significant results. Refer to Table 3.3 for full list of variables included in the model. Admin = Administration; Cmd = Command; Educ = Education; Eng = Engineering; IT = Information Technology; Mgmt = Management; Misc = Miscellaneous; Svcs = Services; USAF = U.S. Air Force.

in which a characteristic was statistically significant in more than one model, but the magnitude of the effect varied. All the magnitude values are available for review in Appendix A.

Turning our attention to interpretation, some types of personnel might be disciplined (suspended) before being terminated,[4] while others instead are terminated without the intermediate step of disciplinary action. Those different performance management strategies may help account for some of our findings. For example, supervisors had a higher probability of disciplinary action, possibly because it is preferable to suspend a supervisor for poor performance or misconduct rather than terminate him or her outright. Conversely,

---

[4] As noted earlier in the report, we observed 14 cases of the personnel both disciplined and terminated during their probationary period.

higher education was associated with a lower probability of disciplinary action, perhaps because new hires with higher education tend to perform well and conduct themselves professionally. Looking at occupations, it is unclear why some MCOs, specifically HR Management and Inventory Management, had a higher probability of disciplinary action during probation, while two other MCOs, Economist and IT Management, had a lower probability of disciplinary action during probation. This could be because STEM personnel are perceived as harder to recruit and thus suspension is used as a corrective strategy before resulting to termination, or perhaps personnel in Economist and IT Management are high performers so that disciplinary actions tend not to be needed.

Characteristics Related to the Probability of Probationary Period Terminations After the First Year, Conditional on Being Terminated

Patterns related to terminations after the first year of probation (but still in the probationary period)[5] are shown in Tables 3.6 and 3.7. The tables' structure resembles that of the preceding tables, with variables without statistically significant results omitted for ease of presentation. Note also that this set of models includes only covered personnel who were terminated during their probationary period rather than the entire group of covered personnel. The smaller group included in the analysis—just under 3,500 personnel—may be one explanation why fewer statistically significant patterns were observed. A summary of findings follows:

- factors related to a higher probability of probationary period termination after the first year:
  - **personal attributes**, specifically having some college education or more education
  - **organizational characteristics**, specifically working in the Hawaii LPA and working at Defense Finance and Accounting Svcs or Defense Logistics Agency
  - **occupations**, specifically MCO/non-STEM occupations and the Logistics Management occupation.
- factors related to a lower probability of probationary period termination after the first year:
  - **organizational characteristics**, specifically working at Defense Commissary Agency or DoD Education Activity
  - **occupation**, specifically the Sales Store Clerical occupation.

Based on percentage point difference (0.10 percentage points or greater), all the factors listed above have a relatively large association with the probability of termination after the first year.

A look at differences in nonoccupational characteristics across the three models again indicated that the majority of results were the same in terms of statistical significance and the direction of effects. We did note four differences, one related to race and three to organization. In Model 2, Other race was significantly associated with a lower probability of first-year probation termination than White race. In different models, working in U.S. Army Reserve Command or DoD Education Activity was either significantly associated with a lower probability of first-year probation termination or not significant. Finally, Defense Logistics Agency was significantly associated with a higher probability of first-year probation termination in two of the three model specifications. There were also some instances in which a characteristic was statistically significant in more than one model, but the magnitude of the effect varied. All the magnitude values are available for review in Appendix A.

Thinking about these results may be interpreted, it is possible that supervisors either take more time to evaluate probationary employees with higher levels of education and those in MCOs or give them more time

---

[5] We use this terminology because not all probationary period terminations after the first year occurred in the second year. In some instances, a termination was observed in the third year of employment for individuals within a STRL demonstration project.

TABLE 3.6

Regression Analysis Summary: Characteristics Related to the Probationary Period Terminations After the First Year, Conditional on Being Terminated, Model 1

Variable	Direction of Effect	Magnitude of at Least 0.10 Percentage Points
Education level (referent group: no college)		
Some college	Positive	Yes
Bachelor's degree or higher	Positive	Yes
LPA (referent group: all other LPAs [including rest of the United States])		
Hawaii	Positive	Yes
Subagency (referent group: all other subagencies)		
Fourth Estate		
Defense Commissary Agency	Negative	Yes
Defense Finance and Accounting Svcs	Positive	Yes
Defense Logistics Agency	Positive	Yes
DoD Education Activity	Negative	Yes

SOURCE: Authors' analysis of DMDC data.

NOTES: Number of observations for covered personnel = 3,485. Statistically significant results are significant at p-value < .05. Table only includes statistically significant results. Refer to Table 3.2 for full list of variables included in the model. Svcs = Services.

TABLE 3.7

Regression Analysis Summary: Occupational Characteristics Related to the Probationary Period Terminations After the First Year, Conditional on Being Terminated, All Models

Variable	Direction of Effect	Magnitude of at Least 0.10 Percentage Points
Model 1		
MCO/non-STEM	Positive	Yes
Model 3		
Administrative		
Logistics Mgmt	Positive	Yes
Clerical		
Sales Store Clerical	Negative	Yes

SOURCE: Authors' analysis of DMDC data.

NOTES: Number of observations for covered personnel: Model 1 = 3,485 and Model 3 = 3,485. Statistically significant results are significant at p-value < .05. Table only includes statistically significant results. Refer to Table 3.3 for full list of variables included in the model. Model 2 results not included because none of the occupation variables were statistically significant in that model specification. Mgmt = Management.

to turn around poor performance before initiating a probationary period termination. Conversely, it may be easier to evaluate quickly newly appointed personnel working at Defense Commissary Agency or DoD Education Activity and those in the Sales Store Clerical occupation—or it could be that these personnel may be more likely to fail to meet conditions of employment, such as obtaining a required certification or a negative drug test.

A Look Across Probationary Period Termination and Disciplinary Action Outcomes

In this section, we report the results of a look across outcomes. This was intended to identify when certain personal attributes, organizations, or occupations were statistically significant in multiple instances, such as being significantly associated with both a higher probability of probationary period terminations and probationary period disciplinary actions (suspensions). We also looked for cases in which the significance of the effect varied (i.e., statistically significant for one outcome but not another) and when the direction of significance change (e.g., positive in one instance and negative in another). For all but occupational characteristics, we focused on the Model 1 (main model) results and for occupations we considered findings across all three models. The results of this exercise are summarized in Tables 3.8 and 3.9. In the tables, shading highlights the factors that were statistically significant for both outcomes. Table 3.8 shows the intersections of probationary period termination and probationary period disciplinary action findings, and Table 3.9 shows the intersections of probationary period termination and first-year probationary period termination findings. As a reminder, the direction of the finding (i.e., lower or higher probability) is in relation to a referent group, such as White for race, Fourth Estate for service/component, and all other subagencies for subagencies.

Looking first at the comparison of probationary period termination and probationary period disciplinary action findings (Table 3.8), factors related to a higher probability of both outcomes include

- **personal attributes**, specifically being Black and being in a position covered by a bargaining unit
- **organizational characteristics**, specifically working at Air Force Materiel Command, U.S. Army Reserve Command, U.S. Fleet Forces Command, or U.S. Pacific Fleet.

Factors related to a lower probability of both outcomes include

- **personal attributes**, specifically being female and having at least a bachelor's degree
- **organizational characteristics**, specifically working at the Defense Contract Management Agency
- **occupations**, specifically STEM occupation (either MCO or non-MCO), and working in the Economist, Mechanical Engineering, and Miscellaneous Clerk and Assistant occupations.

It is useful to contemplate what might be driving these findings, in part because different reasons might require different responses. For example, if Black personnel have higher probabilities of probationary period termination and disciplinary action due to discrimination, the corrective actions that DoD implements would differ from those taken if those outcomes were instead based on valid reasons. For employees with at least a bachelor's degree, it is possible that additional education is associated with higher performance, thereby reducing the need for probationary period terminations or disciplinary actions. Another potential explanation for our results is that STEM personnel are in high demand and difficult to replace—therefore, supervisors might prefer to address performance or conduct issues for these personnel with informal feedback instead of formal adverse action.

Finally, there are two instances in which the significance of the two outcomes is in different directions: for those in the HR Management occupation, the probability of a probationary period termination was lower, but the probability of disciplinary action was higher; and conversely, for those working at Defense Commissary Agency, the probability of a probationary period termination was higher, but the probability of probationary period disciplinary action was lower. The latter case might reflect an organizational preference not to use suspensions for probationary employees.

Turning to Table 3.9, the comparison of probationary period terminations overall and probationary period terminations after the first year revealed that there were no factors included in the regression models that were related to either a higher probability of both outcomes or a lower probability of both outcomes.

TABLE 3.8
Combined Summary of Probationary Period Termination and Probationary Period Disciplinary Action Findings

		Probability of Probationary Period Disciplinary Action		
		Lower and Significant	**Higher and Significant**	**Not Significant**
Probability of probationary period termination	**Lower and significant**	**Personal attribute** • Female • Bachelor's degree or higher **Service, component, or agency** • Defense Contract Management Agency **Occupation** • MCO/STEM • Non-MCO/STEM • Economist • Mechanical Eng • Misc Clerk and Assistant	**Occupation** • HR Mgmt	**Personal attribute** • Age 40 and older • Asian race • Hispanic ethnicity • Veteran • Some college • Mid-level pay grade at entry • Senior-level pay grade at entry **Service, component, or agency** • Air Force • Army • Navy • Army National Guard units (Title 32) **Location** • Hawaii LPA **Occupation** • MCO/non-STEM • Contracting • Education and Training • Technician • Financial Admin and Program • Fire Protection and Prevention • General Business and Industry • Logistics Mgmt; Security Admin
	Higher and significant	**Service, component, or agency** • Defense Commissary Agency	**Personal attribute** • Black • Bargaining unit **Service, component, or agency** • Air Force Materiel Cmd • U.S. Army Reserve Cmd • U.S. Fleet Forces Cmd • U.S. Pacific Fleet	**Personal attribute** • American Indian or Alaska Native • Other race • Disability **Service, component, or agency** • Air Combat Cmd • Army Corps of Engineers • Army Medical Cmd • Naval Air Systems Cmd • Naval Facilities Engineering Cmd • Naval Medical Cmd • Navy Installations Cmd • U.S. Marine Corps • DoD Education Activity **Occupation** • Misc Warehousing and Stock Handling • Nurse
	Not significant	**Occupation** • IT Mgmt	**Personal attribute** • Supervisor **Location** • Boston LPA **Occupation** • Inventory Mgmt	All other personal, organizational, and occupational factors in the regression models

SOURCE: Authors' analysis of DMDC data.

NOTES: Statistically significant results are significant at p-value < .05. Referent groups include male, younger than age 40, White race, no college, non-Hispanic ethnicity, no known disability, non-veteran, not being a bargaining unit member, entry-level pay grade at entry, Fourth Estate, and, for occupation group, non-MCO/non-STEM. For LPA, agency, and specific occupations, the referent group is all others. The Accounting occupation was associated with a significantly higher probability of termination but dropped out of disciplinary actions models because of multicollinearity. The table does not include significant findings for unnamed occupations or "missing" categories. Shading is used to highlight the factors that were statistically significant for both outcomes. Admin = Administration; Cmd = Command; Eng = Engineering; IT = Information Technology; Mgmt = Management; Svcs = Services.

TABLE 3.9
Combined Summary of Probationary Period Termination and Probationary Period Termination Timing Findings

		Probability of Probationary Period Termination After First Year, Conditional on Being Terminated	
		Lower and Significant / **Higher and Significant**	**Not Significant**
Probability of probationary period termination	**Lower and significant**	*Lower and Significant:* None of the personal, organizational, and occupational factors included in the regression models. *Higher and Significant:* **Personal attribute** • Some college • Bachelor's degree or higher **Service, component, or agency** • Army National Guard units (Title 32) **Location** • Hawaii LPA **Occupation** • MCO/non-STEM • Logistics Mgmt	**Personal attribute** • Age 40 and older • Female • Asian race • Hispanic ethnicity • Veteran • Mid-level pay grade at entry • Senior-level pay grade at entry **Service, component, or agency** • Air Force • Army • Navy • Defense Contract Mgmt Agency **Occupation** • MCO STEM • Non-MCO STEM • Contracting • Economist • Education and Training Technician • Financial Admin and Program • Fire Protection and Prevention • General Business and Industry • HR Mgmt • Mechanical Eng • Misc Clerk and Assistant • Security Admin
	Higher and significant	*Lower and Significant:* **Service, component, or agency** • Defense Commissary Agency • DoD Education Activity. *Higher and Significant:* None of the personal, organizational, and occupational factors included in the regression models	**Personal attribute** • Black • American Indian or Alaska Native • Other race • Disability • Bargaining unit **Service, component, or agency** • Air Combat Cmd • Air Force Materiel Cmd • Army Corps of Engineers • Army Medical Cmd • Army Reserve Cmd **Service, component, or agency** • Naval Air Systems Cmd • Naval Facilities Engineering Cmd • Naval Medical Cmd • Navy Installations Cmd • U.S. Fleet Forces Cmd • Marine Corps • U.S. Pacific Fleet **Occupation** • Accounting • Misc Warehousing and Stock Handling • Nurse
	Not significant	*Lower and Significant:* **Occupation** • Sales Store Clerical. *Higher and Significant:* **Service, component, or agency** • Defense Finance and Accounting Svcs • Defense Logistics Agency	All other personal, organizational, and occupational factors included in the regression models

SOURCE: Authors' analysis of DMDC data.

NOTES: Statistically significant results are significant at p-value < .05. Referent groups include male, younger than age 40, White race, no college, non-Hispanic ethnicity, no known disability, non-veteran, not being a bargaining unit member, entry-level pay grade at entry, Fourth Estate, and, for occupation group, non-MCO/non-STEM. For LPA, agency, and specific occupations, the referent group is all others. Army National Guard units (Title 32) were associated with a significantly lower probability of termination but dropped out of termination timing models due no probationary period terminations beyond first year. The table does not include significant findings for unnamed occupations or "missing" categories. Shading is used to highlight the factors that were statistically significant for both outcomes. Admin = Administration; Cmd = Command; Eng = Engineering; IT = Information Technology; Mgmt = Management; Svcs = Services.

The majority of characteristics included in the models were only significantly associated with one outcome at most. Higher education was again significantly associated with two outcomes. Specifically, having at least some college was statistically associated with a lower probability of probationary period termination but, conditional on being terminated, a higher probability of being terminated after the first year. One potential reason for this is that if, as suggested earlier in this chapter, those with more education have a higher level of performance, then supervisors may be giving more highly educated personnel the benefit of the doubt and delay a termination decision as long as possible.

CHAPTER FOUR

Removal Case Analysis

This chapter features a summary of our in-depth qualitative review of removal cases for individuals terminated during their probationary periods in the time frame of interest. We cover how the cases were selected and analyzed and describe findings related to case file contents, reasons for termination, case trajectories, and our comparison of probationary period terminations occurring during the first year with those after the first year. In doing so, this chapter addresses the following required report element:

> (5) Discussion of cases in which DoD made a determination to remove an employee during the second year of his or her probationary period, including a comparison of those removals to first-year removals.

Case Selection

DCPAS staff used a purposive sampling approach to select termination cases for us to review. First, DCPAS staff examined the full list of terminated personnel from our analysis of probationary period terminations through December 31, 2020, and noted how often the same supervisor of record was associated with multiple termination actions. The RAND study team and DCPAS staff agreed to use this factor as a basis for case selection, reasoning that a supervisor involved in multiple cases would be a good candidate to interview not only to discuss a specific case but for broader insights about termination actions during probation (e.g., challenges and promising practices). Among the 3,558 termination actions that DCPAS reviewed,[1] 143 supervisors of record were associated with two or more actions, covering 395 actions in total. More than half of the actions—1,863 actions—had a unique supervisor of record (i.e., the supervisor was associated with only one case during the covered time frame). Finally, 1,300 cases did not have a supervisor of record within the administrative data file. Those cases were excluded from the sample because it was unclear whether a supervisor would be available for us to interview as part of our qualitative assessment of the use and utility of the two-year probationary period.

After focusing primarily—but not solely—on actions carried out by repeat users of probationary period terminations, DCPAS then sought to vary the selection of cases across the military services and Fourth Estate, then by subagency and occupation. The results of our preliminary statistical analyses using data through June 30, 2020, were also taken into consideration to ensure that factors that emerged as statistically significant were reflected in the full sample. For example, the sample includes termination actions associated with those in positions covered by bargaining units and with personnel working in subagencies that had a higher likelihood of using probationary periods in general or second-year probation terminations in particular. The sample included personnel with many of the personal, job, and organizational factors related to a

---

[1]   This number of terminations differs from the figures provided in Chapter Two because DCPAS had to request additional data from DMDC for the purposes of both this case file review and OSC/EEOC appeal elements of the study. During that process, additional personnel were included in the list provided to DCPAS. DCPAS, DMDC, and RAND could not identify the cause for these additional personnel being included. Ultimately, the cases selected all pertained to covered personnel (i.e., those with an SES or competitive service appointment).

higher likelihood of termination during the probationary period, with the notable exception being that none of the cases were from the Accounting or Nurse occupations.

Ultimately, DCPAS selected 48 removal cases out of 3,558 cases (1.3 percent) for us to review[2] and requested that the employing agencies provide the case files with appropriate redactions to DCPAS so that they could be transmitted to us. Of these 48 cases, the employing agencies were unable to locate materials for four cases, and one case file we received did not align with the data, resulting in a final analysis sample of 43 cases.

Descriptive Overview of Cases

In this section, we describe the 43 cases we received and reviewed in depth and summarize the basic characteristics of the five cases for which files were requested but unavailable for our review. To protect the identities of those terminated, we do not identify specific Fourth Estate agencies in our discussion, and, in some cases, when we share excerpts from case files, we redact precise case details.

For the 43 cases we analyzed, the average time to termination was 371 days, or just over one year. About half of the removals (22 out of 43 cases) occurred during the first year of probation, with time to termination for these cases averaging 197 days, just over six months. The remaining 21 cases involved terminations during the second year of probation (or later, in one instance of one Navy probationary employee required to serve a three-year probationary period). Time to termination for these second-year cases averaged 552 days or just over 1.5 years. The five cases that DCPAS requested but did not receive were split between three first-year and two second-year terminations.

With respect to demographics, 30 of the 43 probationary employees whose cases we reviewed were male (70 percent) and 13 were female (30 percent). Twenty-one were White employees, 15 were Black employees, and seven were of another race. Three were of Hispanic ethnicity. Thirteen cases involved people with disabilities, including six cases of veterans with disabilities. A total of 15 cases involved veterans, including the six with disabilities and nine others. The average age of the terminated probationers was 38, with 20 cases involving individuals ages 40 or older and 23 concerning personnel younger than age 40. Most of the cases we reviewed (25 cases, or 58 percent) involved individuals with no college education. The five cases that were requested but not received all concerned male personnel, three of whom had a bachelor's degree or higher education, and three of whom were veterans. Their races, ethnicities, and ages displayed no pattern.

The cases we reviewed were split relatively evenly between the Air Force (12 cases), Army (ten cases), Navy (11 cases), and the Fourth Estate (ten cases). Two cases we did not receive were Fourth Estate cases, one was Air Force, one was Army, and one was Navy. Most cases involved probationary employees who were in entry-grade positions (25 cases, or 58 percent), a little over a quarter (12 cases) concerned mid-grade position personnel, and the remainder (six cases) pertained to personnel in positions with unknown grade levels. None of the cases we reviewed involved senior-grade personnel. The cases concerned a mix of blue-collar personnel (20 cases) and white-collar personnel (23 cases), Most of these white-collar personnel were in administrative, clerical, or technical occupations. Four cases (all white-collar personnel) concerned individuals in mission-critical STEM occupations and two pertained to individuals in mission critical non-STEM occupations. Of the five cases we did not receive, four were white-collar cases, two of which were mission critical non-STEM personnel. Three of the five cases concerned entry-level personnel.

---

[2] Initially the plan was to review 50 cases in depth, but two of the cases that DCPAS selected were outside our analysis period. For one, the individual's termination occurred within our analysis time frame but was for an appointment beginning before that time frame. For the other individual, his or her termination was in our time frame, but it was the individual's second appointment within this time frame. As we explained in Chapter Two, we made an analytic decision to focus on first appointments in the covered time frame and dropped later appointments from our analysis.

Analytical Approach

We began by documenting which cases we received and confirming that the case files we received matched on key characteristics to the data (e.g., by confirming that the agency and occupation mentioned in the case files corresponding to a certain scrambled Social Security number aligned with the data for that scrambled number). We then catalogued the contents of each case file and developed a semistructured template to capture relevant information we anticipated being able to extract from each case package. We proceeded in an iterative fashion, reviewing a small number of test cases at first, having multiple analysts review the same case, and adjusting the template before expanding to a larger number of cases, repeating the process, and ultimately covering the full set of cases. Overall, approximately one in seven cases was reviewed by multiple analysts as a consistency check.

In addition to the contents of the package, we collected the following elements, when available, from each case file:

- reason for termination
- employee recourse offered or taken
- amount and timing of warning from supervisor to probationer
- any documented positive feedback from supervisor
- whether a performance review was included in the case file
- documentation of leadership review or sign-off on termination
- timeline from appointment to termination (and any documented subsequent actions).

After reviewing the case files, we synthesized the information we captured in the template to identify key themes and patterns, both in terms of the structure of the case files (e.g., whether they tend to contain the same materials and degree of documentation) and the substance of the termination cases (e.g., reasons for termination, typical timeline). We considered the extent to which the case files included items required by statutes and DoD or component regulations regarding probation. For example, the minimum requirements of what must be given to the probationary employee (e.g., timing and nature of notice of the proposed termination, deadline to respond, appeal rights) are explained in 5 CFR 315.804 or 315.805, depending on whether the termination is based on post- or pre-appointment reasons, and DoD Administrative Instruction 8, which instructs supervisors to coordinate with HR or Labor Management Employee Relations (LMER) and requires that the termination notice include documentation of an individual's performance or conduct deficiencies.[3] Finally, we paid particular attention to exploring the characteristics of terminations that occurred during the second year, given congressional direction in the FY 2020 NDAA that our review should include a discussion of these cases.

Limitations

The principal limitation of our termination case analysis is the small sample of cases we reviewed. Though the cases were selected in a purposive manner to capture a variety of experiences across DoD, and they do capture important variation by agency, occupation, and timing of termination, they were not selected at random. This means they are not representative of the full population of terminated probationary employees, and, at times

---

[3] 5 CFR 315.804, Termination of Probationers for Unsatisfactory Performance or Conduct, last updated December 1, 2005; 5 CFR 315.805, Termination of Probationers for Conditions Arising Before Appointment, last updated February 7, 2008; and DoD Administrative Instruction 8, "Disciplinary and Adverse Actions," December 16, 2016, incorporating Change 1, February 9, 2022.

the demographics associated with our termination cases differ notably from those of the overall population. For example, relative to the demographics for all terminations (Table 2.1), White personnel are underrepresented in our termination cases and Black personnel and those with a reported disability are overrepresented.

Some of this under- and overrepresentation was an intentional effort to focus on categories of personnel that our statistical analysis flagged as having a higher likelihood to experience termination during the probationary period. Despite that being our sampling objective, some statistically significant characteristics were not included in our termination case sample, most notably those in Accounting and Nurse occupations. The cases shed light on DoD policies and practices with respect to probationary terminations, and we draw on them to identify major themes, promising practices, and practices of possible concern that may merit further investigation. However, we do not know how representative the cases we reviewed are of the full set of probationary period terminations in our time frame of interest (November 26, 2015 through December 31, 2020). Findings from the case analysis should be considered alongside additional evidence drawn from our statistical analysis and interviews with relevant stakeholders.

Additionally, we are limited by observing only cases that resulted in terminations. We are unable to determine whether or how often individuals who would have been terminated prior to the end of a one-year probationary period are instead retained into the second year and beyond because of flexibilities that the two-year probationary period provides to supervisors and DoD. For example, if an individual was not meeting performance expectations during his or her first year but improved in the second year and was ultimately not terminated, we would not see that case or its trajectory. In other words, the second year of probation may be useful for giving employees time to improve their performance or conduct, but we could not assess that benefit. We also may not observe instances when an individual successfully appealed a termination through internal channels (e.g., by seeking review from a next-level supervisor), because all such occurrences in the cases we reviewed resulted in terminations within DoD. It is possible we could have seen cases with external reviews (e.g., by the MSPB), because DoD would have proceeded with the termination prior to those actions occurring; however, the cases we reviewed also did not include documentation of any successful appeals to external bodies.

Finally, our knowledge of the individual cases is limited to the documentation included in the case files. In many instances, conversations between supervisors and those in their probationary periods are captured in memoranda for the record that are then included in the case files. However, if such conversations were only irregularly documented in writing, or if there were variation in the degree to which those written materials were preserved and included in the terminated probationers case files, our knowledge of the full trajectory of the cases, including any negative or positive feedback provided to the employees over the time of their employment, would be circumscribed.

Case File Contents

We reviewed the documents included in each case file, looking for similarities and differences in what was included and omitted. Case files ranged from a low of five pages to more than 100 pages, and some cases included various memoranda, evidence, and forms, while others had a termination letter and little more documentation. An important caveat is that individual case files we received may not be the entirety of a specific case file accessible by the agency and the employee.

Cross-Case Commonalities

All the cases we reviewed included a memorandum or letter of termination, informing the probationary employee of the action. The memoranda we reviewed were about 1.5 pages to five pages in length. At the minimum, all memoranda include the date of appointment, date of termination, and reason for termination. In some memoranda, the reason for termination is one sentence long, while, in others, it includes the timeline of various transgressions and supervisor responses. The following excerpt, from a Navy termination letter, is typical of how the reason for termination is described:

> The reason for this action is: From [DATE REDACTED], through the date of this letter, you have not reported to work or contacted your supervisor or shop to request and receive approval for leave. You have been charged to unauthorized absence on each scheduled workday. This absence is excessive unauthorized absence.

The memorandum also informs the employee of the rights to which they are entitled: the MSPB and in most, but not all cases, the EEOC for terminations based on a protected class, and OSC for terminations based on whistleblowing. All the memoranda also include contact information for either an individual or an office who can assist the terminated employee with their appeal by providing needed documents and information about regulations and procedure.

In addition to the memorandum or letter which is included in every case file, most files also include the OPM's Standard Form 50 (SF-50), Notification of Personnel Action. This form is included in 31 of the 42 files. Almost all the files include some sort of evidence, such as timesheets documenting excessive leave, drug and alcohol test results, employee discipline summaries or memoranda of record describing various incidents.

Cross-Case Variation

We noted a great deal of variation in terms of the cases' file length and the types of documents included. The variation depends on many factors, including the length of employment, reason for termination, and whether the employee pursued recourse. Other differences, such as whether memoranda of record, correspondence with HR, or sign-off from leadership is included may be due to the more idiosyncratic management styles of the supervisor. There is also the open question of whether the case files we received contain the entirety of the record, or whether some files are missing the types of emails, memoranda, or other evidence that are included in other files.

Some of the main differences are whether performance reviews are included, as they are in ten files, whether there is correspondence with or sign-off from leadership (21 files), whether the legal or regulatory basis for termination is included (nine files), whether a position description, job summary or similar document is included (13 files), whether appeals documents are included, and the amount and type of evidence included.

Another important variation across the military services and Fourth Estate cases is the type of recourse outside the agency's chain of command that is made available to the probationary employee. As required by statute, all the memoranda include reference to the right to an MSPB appeal. All the Navy cases also include OSC and EEO appeal rights. Five cases reference neither OSC nor EEO appeal rights. Of those, one is from a Fourth Estate agency, one from the Air Force, and three from the Army. Four of those involve personnel in bargaining units. Three of the cases simply mention the MPSB appeal, while two of the cases note that cases based on discrimination may be raised in conjunction with MSPB appeals based on marital status or partisan political affiliation. For example, one letter prepared by the Army explains:

> Your discharge during your probationary period is not grievable, and can only be appealed to the U.S. Merit Systems Protection Board if you allege that your discharge was because of discrimination due to marital status or partisan political affiliation. Should you do so, you may also raise issues of discrimination due to race, color, religious, sex, national origin, physical handicap, and/or age.

In addition to these five cases which only mention MSPB appeal rights, the letters in three Air Force terminations (all personnel in positions covered by bargaining units) do not include EEO rights, only OSC and MSPB. Of those, the memorandum of separation, as it is called in the Air Force, for one case explains that the employee may allege discrimination on the basis of an EEOC condition in their MSPB appeal, in addition to claims on the basis of partisan political reasons or marital status. Finally, seven cases, all for personnel in bargaining units, reference MSPB and EEO rights, but not the right to an OSC appeal. This includes four Army, one Air Force, and the two Fourth Estate cases.

Another important distinction between cases is whether the probationary employee is offered an opportunity to contest the termination within the agency's chain of agency. Certain case files contain one of two mechanisms: the right to reply to or rebut the proposed termination or the right to request a review of termination. In two cases, one Army and the other Navy, the probationers were given the right to reply. The language in the former's letter of proposed termination is as follows:

> You have the right to reply to this proposal. You may reply in person, in writing, or both, stating why this proposed action should not be taken. You may submit affidavits and other documentary evidence in support of your reply. Any reply should be made to [. . .], Chief, Supply and Services Division and must be submitted within fifteen (15) calendar days after you receive this letter.

The letter for Navy employees letter is very similar, although those employees were only given ten calendar days to reply. Both Army and Navy employees were also notified of their MSPB, EEO, and OSC appeal rights.

All but one of the Air Force personnel were given the right to request a review of their terminations. The one Air Force individual who was not offered the opportunity to request a review of termination was nevertheless given the right to provide a rebuttal reply to the suspension of access to classified information (a condition of employment), within 72 hours. In the Air Force's memorandum for notice to terminate during probationary period, the 11 other Air Force cases we reviewed all explained that the individual has the right to request review of the termination action. For example, the letter sent to a personnel psychologist said,

> You may request a review of this termination action from the Reviewing Official . . . within three (3) working days from the receipt of this letter. This request must be in writing and must set forth the reasons why you believe this action should not be taken. You may submit affidavits and other evidence in support of your reply. It is important that you exercise this right within the time limits established above, as you have no other right of review of this action. You will be notified of the final decision, in writing, if you request a review. If you do not request a review of this action, you will be terminated as specified in paragraph 1 above.

The amount of time that the individuals being terminated are given to submit their requests differs from case to case, ranging from three to seven days.

Reasons for Termination

At the outset of our analysis, we categorized the reasons for termination, as described in the memoranda or letters for termination, into broad bins. The different types of reasons that an employee was terminated in a probationary period informs many other elements of the analysis. Ultimately, we found that the cases could be put into one of eight bins, some related to performance or ability to perform, others to misconduct, and some involving both performance and misconduct. They are listed in Table 4.1 and discussed in the sections that follow.

Bad Performance or Pattern of Errors

In 11 cases, the individual's termination can be attributed to general poor performance or a series of errors. In some cases, the probationary employee failed to meet production targets over an extended period. For example, the termination memorandum to a Fourth Estate probationary employee explained that, despite

TABLE 4.1

Removal Case Analysis Results: Reasons for Termination

Reason for Termination	Number of Cases
Bad performance or pattern of errors	11
Unacceptable leave usage or tardiness	9
Unacceptable leave usage/tardiness and general bad performance	7
Inability to pass required test or receive certification	5
Severe misconduct on the job	5
Lost access to classified information or areas	3
Positive drug test results	2
Severe misconduct off the job	1

SOURCE: RAND analysis of removal cases provided by DCPAS.

counseling, that individual's average production rate failed to improve and remained at 76 percent, well below the 90-to-100-percent threshold. In other cases, the termination letter describes specific errors. For example, from the memorandum to an Air Force probationary employee:

> Since your appointment, you have exhibited difficulty following Air Force Instructions, and technical data, and you failed to demonstrate the necessary skills, experience, or aptitude to work on critical aircraft flight control actuators. After being trained to disassemble an actuator, on or about [DATE REDACTED], you failed to follow the disassembly instructions found in TO 8A1-8-7-3, when you chose a large wrench to physically force parts off the actuator housing, resulting in the center housing assembly cracking and bending [PART REDACTED]. This part was not repairable and had to be replaced at a cost of approximately [COST REDACTED].

Other cases fall in between these two: neither months of missing performance targets nor a few large mistakes but rather a pattern of sloppy performance is the reason. For example, in a letter to an Air Force probationary employee:

> You have failed to qualify during your probationary period for the following reasons:
>
> a. You show little ability to stay on task and show no initiative to learn the sheet metal trade.
> b. You regularly fail to follow my directives for your required daily activities, such as logging onto cards and staying on task until the end of shift.
> c. I have noted several times that you walk around "ready to leave" (with your backpack on), failing to display attentiveness to your duties.
> d. You regularly delay beginning aircraft maintenance tasks until 20 minutes prior to the end of shift.
> e. You failed to attend several mandatory end of shift discussions for task completions/accomplishments.

Unacceptable Leave Usage or Tardiness

The probationary employee's unacceptable leave usage or regular tardiness is the stated reason for termination in nine cases. An example of how this reason or termination is described in a termination letter follows:

During your probationary period, you have failed to meet management's attendance expectations. On [DATE], you were counseled on your leave usage, since that time your leave usage has not improved.

In certain letters or memoranda, specific dates of tardiness or absent without official leave (AWOL) are included as well. Typical case file evidence for probationary employees terminated for this reason include timesheets, memoranda for the record detailing absence or tardiness on specific occasions, and lists of dates where employee missed work.

Unacceptable Leave Usage/Tardiness and General Bad Performance

In our analysis we found that seven cases mentioned misconduct in the form of inappropriate leave usage or chronic tardiness in conjunction with performance issues, which quite understandably may go hand in hand. For example, the memorandum to an Air Force probationary employee states the following:

I have determined that you do not possess the qualities and characteristics essential to providing continued satisfactory service. Your actions indicate you cannot be trusted to carry-out your duties in a professional manner. As such, your termination promotes the efficiency of the service. The specific reasons for my determination are as follows:

a. In [DATE], you were tasked with completing a flightline noise service. . . . As of the date of this notification, that survey is still not complete.

b. On [DATE], you were tasked with investigating potential exposure of Beryllium. . . . However, you never conducted the survey nor provide[d] the requested update. . . .

c. On [DATE], you were tasked with establishing a plan to minimize exposure to wood dust particles at the [LOCATION]. . . . As of the date of this notification, you still have not completed those tasks.

d. On [DATE], you and I discussed your habitual tardiness, at which time we established a schedule of 0700-1630, Monday through Friday. On [DATE], you reported to work at 0930, without having previously notified me of your late arrival or requesting leave for this time. When I confronted you about coming to work late again, your raised your voice at me, saying, "I don't want to be bothered by anyone," or words to that effect. On [DATE], you again showed up late for work, again without previously notifying me that you were going to be late or requesting leave for this time. When we met on [DATE], I expressed my expectation that you strictly adhere to this schedule unless you are in an approved leave status. Your actions have failed to meet my expectations.

Inability to Pass Required Test or Receive Certification

In five of the cases we reviewed, employees were terminated for failure to pass a required test or receive required certification. Three of the cases involved security guards who failed the initial physical agility test that is a condition of employment and were terminated soon thereafter.

Severe Misconduct on the Job

In five of the cases we reviewed, the probationary employee was terminated for what can be considered severe misconduct unrelated to job performance. In the cases we categorized as severe misconduct on the job, the individual was terminated for forgery, abusive language (in two cases), insubordination, or threatening another employee.

Lost Access to Classified Information or Areas

In three cases, the probationary employee was terminated because of lost access to classified information or secure areas that was required for employment. The individuals all lost access for different reasons: a failed drug test, history of criminal conduct, and, in one complicated situation, the inability to locate the individual's naturalization certificate. An example of a termination letter in this type of case follows:

> In making my decision to terminate your employment from Federal service, I considered the seriousness of the charge in relation to your duties. As [JOB TITLE REDACTED], you are responsible for scheduling appointments, taking phone messages for providers, and directing callers to the to the appropriate clinic or department. The majority of your duties require that you verify patient identities using a variety of personally identifiable information, such as Social Security numbers and dates of birth. Given the restrictions on your IT network access and suspended security clearance, you are unable to carry out any of those functions. Considering the fact that the probationary period is a final and highly significant step in the examining process, and there is no way to determine when you will [be] able to resume your responsibilities, if ever, I have concluded that you are not suitable for continued employment with the Federal service.

Positive Drug Test Results

In two cases, the reason for termination was that the probationary employee failed a drug test. As noted in the above section, one individual in our case review was terminated for losing access to classified information, which was due to a failed drug test. However, in that case, the proximate cause for the termination is the lost access, not the drug test.

Severe Misconduct off the Job

Finally, in one case, an employee was arrested and charged with driving under the influence, drug possession, and resisting a police officer. In explaining why this merited termination, the notice of proposed termination explained,

> b. Not only did you refuse to comply with the orders of the German police but you were also away from your place of duty without permission, during your duty hours, when the police stopped you
>
> c. As an American working in a foreign country on behalf of the United States you have a higher duty of care than you might otherwise have. Your individual actions reflect on all of those working and living here.

Case Trajectories

Overall, the average time from appointment date to termination date across the 43 cases was 371 days, or about a year, with the typical (i.e., median) case resulting in a termination just under the one-year mark (361 days). A breakdown by six-month intervals of the probationary period follows:

- First six months of employment: ten cases
- Between six months and one year: 12 cases
- Between one year and 1.5 years: 12 cases
- After 1.5 years through end of probationary period: nine cases (with one instance of an employee required to serve a three-year probationary period who was terminated in the third year).

Prior Warnings from Supervisor

In almost all cases, the termination notice and accompanying memorandum informing the employee of termination is not the first time that the employee is alerted to concerns with that individual's conduct, performance, or ability to carry out job duties. However, we observed variation in whether prior warnings and notifications were formally documented and communicated in writing to the probationary employees, or whether they were verbal, sometimes documented in contemporaneous memoranda for the record written by the supervisor and preserved in the employee's file, and other times simply noted in the letter of termination that such conversations had occurred. Moreover, at times, documentation provided to the employee over the course of employment explicitly noted that the employee is subject to a two-year probationary period and warned that certain actions could result in termination; and, other times, it did not.

One case with repeated, formal documentation of incidents and explicit warnings that could lead to termination concerns an individual employed by the Air Force. Beginning about two months after the individual's appointment, incidents of tardiness and performance issues are documented in contemporaneous memoranda, at least some of which appear to have been provided to the individual at the time. A written record of a face-to-face progress review states: "Your probationary period lasts two years from your hire date. It is imperative you work well with your associates. I am concerned about the matter of your suitability to fulfill the duties as a civil servant budget analyst in this work environment." Incidents persist, and the employee is warned a few months later that "[any] negative display of conduct may result in disciplinary action," and again three months later that failing to seek approval for work schedule changes "could result in admonishment and termination." This last warning occurred after the individual's supervisor had already submitted a package of documentation seeking the individual's termination.

A case that proceeded on a faster timeline but that included a similar volume of prior warnings concerns a contract representative for a Fourth Estate agency terminated about four months after the individual's hire date. When the probationary employee began accumulating AWOL time shortly after appointment, the supervisor wrote in an email to the employee: "To clarify, as a newly hired employee, your employment status is probationary. During this two-year probationary period, you are being evaluated for fitness for Federal Service and may be subject to removal."

In another case, an HR assistant in the Army was alerted in a memorandum about less than two months prior to termination that continued poor performance could result in termination, although it does not explicitly note that the employee remained in probationary status. Specifically, the memorandum stated:

> This memorandum of counseling is intended to impress upon you the seriousness of your actions and is considered reasonable, equitable, and fully warranted. It is also considered to be a corrective measure and necessary to promote the efficiency of the service. Failure to correct this behavior may result in further disciplinary action, up to and including removal.

This case involved an employee who had initially been appointed to a different branch and subsequently promoted to a new branch, and there is no documentation provided with respect to performance or conduct in the first year of employment. According to a memorandum issued immediately before termination and the notice of termination itself, mistakes, failure to complete tasks, and conduct issues (e.g., use of cell phone use during work hours) were occurring for the duration of the time in the second year, documented in several emails and memoranda for the record written by the supervisor.

One example of alluding to past counseling but not including written documentation was for a painter in the Navy, who was terminated well into the second year of probation, and whose termination letter referenced having been "counseled on your leave usage." In this case, about eight months lapsed between this counseling and termination.

In some cases, a reprimand or notification follows shortly after a notable incident that precipitates the termination, and might be considered a precursor to the termination itself, as opposed to a warning that persistent poor conduct or performance would result in such a termination. These tend to align with the terminations resulting from severe misconduct on or off the job, or other such discrete events as failing a drug test, physical agility test, certification exam, or a loss of a clearance. For example, after communicating a threat to harm a supervisor to a colleague, an Army technician received a Departmental Counseling Form indicating that "threats or acts of violence . . . can or will lead to disciplinary actions up to and including termination of employment." That same date, the supervisor submitted a memorandum seeking the employee's removal, and the termination occurred about a month later. In another case of threatening a colleague, an employee was immediately placed on administrative leave and notified of it and terminated soon thereafter. In two cases, one involving off-the-job misconduct and another the loss of a clearance, the employees were first issued a notice of proposed termination and provided an opportunity to rebut the charges within a certain period, and then ultimately terminated.

On some occasions, clear-cut terminations did not include prior warning or notification given to the probationary employee at all (at least not present in the written documentation in the files we received); however, in the cases of failed drug tests and failed physical agility tests, the requirements of continued employment were well-established at the time the individuals were appointed, and language related to these requirements typically was included in the case files.

Despite the general pattern of repeated warnings and documentation for cases aside from those entailing clear-cut incidents that quickly let to termination, this was not universally true. For example, in the case of an Air Force mechanic, the employee was there for nearly a year, and the case package does not provide contemporaneous accounts or documentation of communication with the employee prior to the letter of termination.

Prior Positive Feedback

Most cases we received contained little in the way of documented positive feedback to the probationary employee. Typically, individuals either received negative feedback beginning not long after they started their appointments, with variation in the pace that the case escalated to termination, or no documented feedback at all initially. For second-year terminations with limited documentation of ongoing issues in the first year, we were unable to rule out the possibility that there was positive feedback early on but that case files only document factors and events from when the employment situations started to sour.

In nine cases, however, there is some evidence of prior positive feedback included in the case files, typically also interspersed with critical feedback. Four of these cases involved employees who reached the one-year mark, three fell just short of it (terminated within two weeks of reaching one year), and one of the others was a first-year termination resulting from a failed drug test. One warehouse worker in the Fourth Estate was told that a month earlier in the individual's tenure when he or she met output benchmarks "shows you have what it takes to be successful" before subsequently falling below benchmarks repeatedly and ultimately being terminated well into the second year of probation. A Navy IT probationary employee received some comments about showing "great progress" on one objective and "steady progress" on another in what was otherwise a decidedly mixed performance review in FY 2019 that preceded the individual's termination in the next FY.

One Navy air mechanic earned positive reviews around the six-month mark—"Employee is engaged and has the desire and drive to move forward, supervisor speaks very well of the employee"—before a series of absences and AWOL time resulted in termination. In another case involving a training instructor employed by the Air Force, the existence of some positive feedback along the way ("Great job, just have some small areas to improve upon") was used as supporting evidence to rebut charges by the terminated employee of bias on the part of an evaluator whose other reviews of the probationary employee contributed to the decision to terminate for "numerous instances of maltraining and maltreatment of your students." These incidents were documented in extensive student evaluations included in the instructor's case file.

Supervisor Correspondence with Leadership or Other Parties Prior to Termination

A little under half of case files include some documentation indicating correspondence with or approval from another individual or office within the agency, whether a next-level supervisor, HR, legal, or employee relations personnel. These communications range from formal processes seeking sign-off on the termination to informal requests for recommendations on how to handle an employee to post-termination affirmations of termination actions following a request for reconsideration by the terminated employee. We describe this last category in the "Documentation of Recourses Pursued Post-Termination" section later in this chapter. Here we describe types of pre-termination communications and processes.

At the more formal end of the spectrum, in the case of the Air Force instructor described above, prior to moving forward with the termination, both Judge Advocate General and Labor Law Field Support Center staff reviewed case materials and agreed that the reasons given for the proposed termination were adequate from a legal standpoint. The Judge Advocate General letter is illuminating and demonstrates the greater degree of flexibility provided to agencies to terminate personnel during the probationary period:

> [Employee's] failure to attain a satisfactory progression through the instructor evaluation is objectively clear. What is less so, is the time-line for this progression. That being said, [employee] is a probationary employee and the probationary employee status is designed to give the agency an opportunity to assess the cultural suitability of the employee before their full employment property rights are vested. [Employee] appears as a most unsympathetic figure for whom the perceptions align not in his favor. These accusations are quite thin but noisy like a shallow stream. It is worth noting that any one of these offenses would, alone, warrant only a counseling or reprimand at worst.

One Fourth Estate agency that employed two of the probationary employees whose cases we reviewed appears to use a formal case management system for documenting offenses, seeking disciplinary actions (including termination), and obtaining internal sign-offs prior to moving forward with termination. In the cases we reviewed, a case file is created that contains the following input fields:

- case information, including the specialist assigned to the case, the employee's supervisor's name, date assigned, date case closed, and case type (e.g., discipline)
- action proposed and LMER review of the proposed action (note that this field was not completed in the cases we reviewed)
- action decided and LMER review of the decided action (note that this field was completed in the cases we reviewed, with "termination during probationary/trial period" marked as the decided action and two LMER specialists in both cases signing off in between the cases' open dates and termination dates)
- description of the offense
- adverse action to Office of General Counsel and sign-off from this office
- case history for employee
- information on grievances, settlements, or appeals.

In both cases we reviewed from this agency, about two to three weeks passed between the opening of the case file and the termination. One case involved a first-year probationer and the other a second-year probationer. Neither case included any documented recourse taken post-termination.

Other examples of documented processes prior to termination include the proposed termination, opportunity to rebut, and Douglas Factors analysis described in the earlier section, an investigation and legal review of a forgery incident by an Army technician that resulted in a recommendation of termination that was acted upon; and a pre-action investigation worksheet completed by a Fourth Estate agency clerk's supervisor that directs the supervisor to contact HR and says, "When it appears that disciplinary action may be warranted, the HR staff can provide you with guidance on the method of conducting a thorough pre-action investigation, including any regulatory or contractual requirements as well as advise you of the supporting documentation that should be obtained."

Among the cases we reviewed, cases with some evidence of communication (e.g., by email) between the supervisors and either leadership or HR, establishing the facts of a case or seeking guidance on how to proceed were about as common as the formal processes outlined above. At times, the roles of the communicating parties are unclear, as is who has ultimate decision authority over whether and when to terminate. An example of checking in to gain approval involved a Navy mechanic whose supervisor wrote to another individual documenting a history of leave abuse, recommending termination, and asking if the other agreed; after a one-word response, "Concur," the supervisor emailed another individual saying, "Please proceed with the removal." In another case, leadership writes back to a supervisor, "Looking at his leave record it certainly supports his termination." In another, "After discussing this with the other General Foremen, we recommend a termination letter at this time." Cases with documented communications to clarify grounds for termination that suggest multiple parties were part of the decision process include an Army clerk, an Air Force mechanic, and a Navy dispatcher. Additionally, in one instance, documentation that followed the termination action indicated that "[employee's] second level supervisor agreed with the proposed penalty of termination."

Documentation of Recourses Pursued Post-Termination

Although all termination cases we reviewed notified terminated employees of their MSPB appeal rights, most notified of OSC and EEO appeal rights, and some included additional options to request reviews within the agency chain of command, very few case files documented instances of employees availing themselves of these options. In the case of MSPB, OSC, and EEOC, it can be reasoned that most terminated probationary employees would not have had valid standing to make a successful appeal to those entities given the narrowly defined grounds for appeal within their purviews. In a selection of a few dozen cases, it is indeed possible that none could have concerned terminations able to be appealed on those grounds. Indeed, the two cases that led to filings with MSPB were dispatched within about a month for lack of jurisdiction (i.e., not related to marital status or political affiliation). In one of those cases, the MSPB decision stated that the employee "Failed to raise a nonfrivolous allegation that the Board has jurisdiction."

Somewhat more common were instances of probationary employees seeking a review of the termination by a next-level supervisor or HR; it was not always clear from case records the role of the individual to whom probationary employees were directed to make their requests for review. We did not review any cases with overturned terminations, although it is possible we would not have received those cases if the termination were never finalized in the first place, or if external appeals were not included in the case files that we received.

Union Involvement

We also observed few instances of documented union involvement or support to employees who were terminated, consistent with the limited number of cases with terminated probationers seeking recourse. In two cases, the American Federation of Government Employees (AFGE) assisted probationary employees with preparing materials seeking to reverse termination decisions, once as part of a pre-termination opportunity to rebut and another time as part of a request for review post-termination by a next-level supervisor. In both cases, the individuals sought and were granted extensions to prepare their replies with AFGE's assistance, although in one of the cases, Navy personnel assert that the rebuttal was never received, and the termination went through (as it could have even if the rebuttal were received).

We note that the data suggest that all but five of the cases we reviewed involved individuals in positions covered by bargaining units; however, there is some question as to whether the probationary employees are covered by these agreements while in probationary status. For example, in one case (that did not actually proceed to a formal complaint to MSPB), there is a document from MSPB suggesting that probationary terminations may not be covered under some collective bargaining agreements: "The Appellant's position is covered under the collective bargaining agreement between the [Fourth Estate Agency] and the National Association of Government Employees. However, this action is not covered under the collective bargaining agreement." In another case that did result in a formal MSPB filing, there is a statement from an LMER Division specialist that "[t]he position from which the Appellant was removed was not covered by a collective bargaining agreement," despite appearing to be covered based on the employee's bargaining unit status on the SF-50 form.

Comparing First and Second Year Terminations

As noted earlier in this chapter, a required element of the review mandated in the FY 2020 NDAA is a discussion of the cases in which DoD decided to remove an individual employee during the second year of his or her probationary period. Among the cases we reviewed, 22 were first-year terminations and 21 were second-year terminations.[4] Across the agencies, the breakdown of year one versus year two cases is about the same—terminations occurred in the first year in five of ten Army cases and Fourth Estate cases, seven of 12 Air Force cases, and five of 11 Navy cases. Table 4.2 includes tabulations of selected demographic characteristics for the first- and second-year termination cases included in our removal case analysis.

For most cases that resulted in terminations within a year, reasons for termination were relatively clear cut (e.g., performance, attendance, or conduct issues that quickly arise), and there was, on average, less documentation of feedback and warnings over time. However, there were exceptions, and those were typically cases entailing a mix of performance and conduct factors leading to termination; for example, in the case of a psychologist terminated shortly before the end of the first year of probation, there is extensive documentation of performance issues that arose during the first year, including a memorandum of concern written by the supervisor to the probationary employee and a point-by-point rebuttal from that employee prior to the employee's eventual termination. Moreover, in the cases we reviewed, there does not appear to be much difference between first- and second-year terminations with respect to whether supervisors corresponded with leadership or others prior to terminating the employee, or whether there was ever any documented positive feedback to the employee (uncommon in general). In addition, a larger share of employees terminated in the first year pursued recourse after the termination (including the two dismissed MSPB cases) than those terminated in their second year of probation.

For terminations that occurred in the second year, there are two main categories of cases: (1) probationary employees who were in their positions for more than one year but were terminated because of a clear incident (e.g., threats, forgery, a failed drug test, or off-the-job arrest) and (2) those who had either ongoing performance or misconduct issues that ultimately culminated in their termination. Our analysis indicates that the first category accounts for six of the second-year termination cases, while the second category accounts for the majority, itself split between performance problems, leave abuse, and a mix of the two. For the six cases

---

4   Note we include the one probationary period termination that happened in the third year of employment in the second-year figure and subsequent first-year and second-year comparisons.

TABLE 4.2

Demographic Characteristics of First- and Second-Year Termination Cases in Case Removal Analysis

Demographic Category	Characteristic	Total Termination Cases	First-Year Termination Cases	Second-Year Termination Cases
	Overall group size	43	22	21
Age				
	Age 40 or older	20	12	8
	Younger than 40	23	10	13
Gender				
	Female	13	9	4
	Male	30	13	17
Race				
	White	21	11	10
	Black	15	5	10
	Asian	2	2	0
	American Indian or Alaska Native	1	0	1
	Hawaiian/Pacific Islander	1	1	0
	Other race	3	3	0
Hispanic ethnicity				
	Hispanic	3	3	0
	Not Hispanic	40	19	21
Veteran				
	Yes	14	7	7
	No	29	15	14
Disability status				
	Yes	13	9	4
	No	30	13	17
Education level				
	No college	25	13	12
	Some college	6	3	3
	Bachelor's degree or higher	12	6	6
Pay grade at appointment				
	Entry-level	25	17	8
	Mid-level	12	5	7
	Senior-level	0	0	0
	Unknown grade	6	0	6

Table 4.2—Continued

Demographic Category	Characteristic	Total Termination Cases	First-Year Termination Cases	Second-Year Termination Cases
In bargaining unit				
	Yes	39	21	18
	No	4	1	3
Service/component				
	Air Force	12	7	5
	Army	10	5	5
	Navy	11	5	6
	Fourth Estate	10	5	5
MCO				
	MCO/STEM	4	3	1
	MCO/non-STEM	2	1	1
	Non-MCO/STEM	0	0	0
	Non-MCO/non-STEM	37	18	19
Type of occupation				
	White collar	23	15	8
	Blue collar	20	7	13

SOURCE: Authors' analysis of removal cases provided by DCPAS.

with incidents arising in the second year, there was no evidence of prior positive feedback, no performance reviews included in their case files, and no recourse taken after termination. One did include a letter or proposed termination and opportunity to rebut, and another had a pre-termination investigation. Three had no prior warnings documented before their termination letters, while the other three had their terminations foreshadowed by the letter of proposed termination, the launch of an investigation into a forgery incident, and in another case, being placed on administrative leave after a threat incident.

The case files for terminations in the second year resulting principally from a pattern of leave abuse or accumulation of AWOL time also tend not to include performance reviews, although they do demonstrate a history of having warned or counseled the employees about their attendance. These terminated probationers did not pursue any recourse, and only one had any history of having earned some modest positive feedback (on performance-related dimensions of the job).

Among those terminated primarily for performance reasons in the second year, five of eight had performance reviews while three did not. Notably, one such review indicated that the employee spent most of the time in training and is "still learning all aspects of the job." This employee and two others earned some positive feedback over the course of their employment. Another was promoted at around the one-year mark. All subsequently saw performance concerns arise or worsen, resulting in termination. In a couple of these cases, there is no documentation of performance during the first year of employment, and we are unable to know if these employees started out strong and then saw their performance erode, or if their performance was unremarkable until it became notably poor. All cases in this category include documentation of prior warnings, and none result in terminated probationers pursuing recourse.

A final set of second-year terminations include three cases with a mix of performance, attendance, and conduct concerns. One concerned a probationary employee with no documentation either positive or negative for the first year and a half of employment, and who appealed the termination to a next-level supervisor (who affirmed it). All three include documentation of prior warnings and conversations between the probationary period employee and his or her supervisor. The case file for an Air Force mechanic was especially detailed in including contemporaneous memos.

A subset of cases with less-than-comprehensive records that might warrant closer scrutiny are those cases that concern probationary employees whose terminations occurred in the second (or third) year and for whom little to no documentation from the first year of employment was included. In these cases, although documentation of concerns, warnings to the individual, and/or communication with leadership prior to the termination may be present as the cases neared termination, the trajectory of these individuals' overall tenure at DoD is unclear from their files. These cases raise a question of whether these individuals were evaluated and found to be performing adequately during the first year, or whether a thorough first-year review, if it had happened, could have surfaced concerns earlier and accelerated the pace of termination.

In addition, we observed few obvious cases of probationary employees terminated in the second year of probation for performance reasons that may have not been able to be detected in the first year because of extensive employee training and rotational requirements. This is despite one rationale for two-year probationary periods offered by managers groups, which is as follows:

> Many federal agencies employ labor forces requiring specialized, technical skills to carry out their duties. New employees must often master broad and complex procedures and policies to meet their agencies' missions, necessitating several months of formal training followed by long periods of on-the-job instruction. [. . .]

> In occupations where training takes substantial time, supervisors may only have a few months upon which to judge employees' on-the-job performance. A longer probationary period allows supervisors to fully assess employees' abilities.[5]

Among the limited set of cases we reviewed, it typically did not appear to be the case that the nature of the work being performed over the first year differs from the long-term nature of the role (e.g., if it were limited to training assignments).

---

[5] Federal Managers Association, "2021 Issue Briefs," 2021.

CHAPTER FIVE

Qualitative Assessment of the Use and Utility of the Probationary Period

In this chapter, we summarize our observations regarding how probation for newly appointed SES and competitive service personnel (during the second year in particular) has been used. We discuss whether supervisors have abused or misused their discretion during the probationary period, note other concerns about the probationary period, and identify the practices that appear helpful and thus are candidates for broader application. We also report perceptions of the impact of the extended probationary period for new hires, including perceptions of how probation has helped DoD and whether it has influenced recruiting, career development, and retention. In doing so, this chapter addresses the following required report elements from the FY 2020 NDAA:

> (3) An analysis of the best practices and abuses of discretion by supervisors and managers of the Department with respect to probationary periods.

> (4) An assessment of the utility of the probationary period prescribed by such section 1599e on the successful recruitment, retention, and professional development of civilian employees of the Department, including any recommendation for regulatory or statutory changes the Secretary determines to be appropriate.

Approach

Findings in this chapter are from the results of our in-depth analysis of 43 removal cases and 31 interviews with DoD HR, legal, and EEO professionals; DoD supervisors; and representatives from both employee unions and a manager association. In some places, we compare our qualitative findings with the results of our statistical analysis. We had hoped to also incorporate EEO appeals data into this analysis, especially in light of statistically significant findings that some protected classes had a higher probability of removal during their probationary period, but the missing data and lack of detail in the data received prevented us from doing so. Also, readers should bear in mind that neither the case sample nor the interview sample is representative, which means we cannot estimate the prevalence of findings, such as a specific type of documentation in case records or opinions about supervisors' approach to probationary period discipline. Rather, the cases and interviews are used to convey a range of practices and viewpoints and provide initial insights about a little-studied topic. With the interviews in particular, our approach was to include observations shared by multiple interview participants (i.e., more than one) when they related to the required report elements or helped to explain the results of our statistical analysis. Additional research is needed to verify how extensively certain practices are used, how widely certain views are held, and whether interviewee perceptions are accurate.

Supervisor-Related Concerns

In this section, we discuss how supervisors may have fallen short in their use of terminations during the probationary period. This part of our analysis includes considering whether supervisors have abused their discretion and other deficiencies that may be less egregious but still warrant improvement.

Abuse of Discretion and Efforts to Mitigate It

Based on the data sources we analyzed, we do not have evidence of abuse of discretion by supervisors with respect to probationary periods. We could also not conclude that such abuse or discrimination was *not* occurring, but we learned about efforts across DoD to avoid misuse of the probationary period and to ensure terminations are for appropriate reasons. In our interviews with DoD HR professionals and supervisors, we consistently heard that supervisors were unable to terminate individuals, even those in their probationary periods, without a review by HR and/or legal counsel. The following descriptions of this process were shared by interviewees from two different agencies:

> With regards to termination, we gather all the documentation from the supervisor and then draft the action and put it through the review process. It is reviewed twice in LER [Labor and Employee Relations]. There is a peer review and then a subject-matter expert/chief level review depending on who is available. Then it goes to the Office of General Counsel for legal sufficiency review before we provide it to the supervisor with instructions on how to issue it.

> When the manager put in a request and tell us the situation, we evaluate it and all the evidence and information regarding the case. Once we review that information, we do a consistency review. Doing the consistency review, we look at other cases within that district that had similar situations. We advise management accordingly on what has been consistent. The reasons for that is to make sure that the employee and the agency is doing the right thing. After that we draft up a proposal memo based on what the manager wants to do. We don't make any decisions. We pretty much provide the information to the manager. We prepare a memo for our legal office of counsel. We provide them with all of our supporting documents so they can provide us with the appropriate legal review. They might come back us with some questions. They let us know what is legally sufficient and we go from there. We don't make any decisions without contacting our legal office.

In some instances, but less consistently, approval by a higher level of management was also required. This seemed to vary by location or by the nature of the infraction—for example, repeat no-shows or a failed drug test.

Another process check mentioned in multiple interviews was the need for the supervisor to provide evidence to justify the termination. Ideally, the evidence would cover not only how the individual fell short in terms of performance or conduct but also what the supervisor did to advise the individual of the deficiency. Examples of such oversight include the following:

> In most cases, we are asking supervisors to document. If they come to us with a performance problem, we are going to want to know when you talked with the employee and did you highlight the deficiency. How long did you wait until the deficiency surfaced again? If we are talking about conduct, did you say this is not okay and if you do it again, it will lead to termination?

> I didn't let a supervisor fire somebody if they had zero evidence. I required at least a modicum of evidence that we could then show to whatever third party that we had a reason to do it. . . . And I think most good EMR [Employee Management Relations] specialists are along the same lines. They're not going to let a supervisor walk in and say, "Billy Bob ain't cutting it," and the EMR specialist gives them a letter and says, "Here, you can give that to him. He's fired." In my experience, that doesn't happen.

Our in-depth review of removal cases provides support that these checks happen, especially with respect to documentation of the poor performance or misconduct. However, as we noted in Chapter Three, case records varied in terms of how supervisor feedback to the probationary employee was provided and documented. In some instances, prior warnings and notifications were formally documented and communicated in writing to the probationary period employees, sometimes the feedback was verbal and then documented for the record and preserved in the employee's file, and in other cases it was simply noted in the letter of termination that such conversations had occurred.

Insufficient Communication Regarding Performance or Conduct Deficiencies

Sometimes the issue regarding supervisor feedback to the probationary employee was not how it was entered into the record but whether it happened at all. Different types of interviewees brought up this concern, including union representatives and HR professionals. One interviewee told us, "I've had managers just handing people their termination letters without even giving them a single negative counseling statement or pointing out a fact that they're making a mistake." Interviewees offered different possible explanations for this type of circumstance, including a lack of training on how to give feedback, supervisor reluctance to have difficult conversations with a subordinate, or more personal or biased reasons. We could not independently verify this type of concern, but we note that insufficient feedback from supervisors is a common issue for employees, both new hires and those with longer tenure. For example, in the 2019 Federal Employee Viewpoint Survey, about one-third of respondents either disagreed with or had a neutral view in response to the statement, "My supervisor provides me with constructive suggestions to improve my job performance." The 2019 survey report shows that this response is an improvement over years past as opposed to a low point.[1]

Termination Action Delays

Although in some cases, delaying a termination until the second year may be appropriate because performance could not be fully assessed in the first year (e.g., due to employee training requirements or a long project work cycle) or because of a need to build a strong evidence base for termination, in other cases, a delayed termination was perceived as problematic. Specifically, we heard in interviews that some supervisors waited until an individual's probationary period was almost over before initiating a termination action. That "wait until the last minute" tendency was regarded with concern because the aforementioned review process requires weeks or even months (in the case of medical professionals), and, in some cases, the individual's probationary period may actually have already ended if the date had not been calculated correctly at the start (this is discussed further in the "Probationary Period Calculation" section later in this chapter). In addition, such an extreme delay is inconsistent with guidance.[2] Specifically, the instruction states,

> Although such discharges may be made at any time during the trial or probationary period, it is important to contact HRD/LMER [Human Resources Directorate/Labor and Management Employee Relations] at least 90 days before the end of the probationary period to ensure the action can be effectuated in a timely fashion.[3]

---

[1] U.S. Office of Personnel Management, *2019 Federal Employee Viewpoint Survey: Governmentwide Management Report*, Washington, D.C., 2019.

[2] DoD Administrative Instruction 8, 2022.

[3] DoD Administrative Instruction 8, 2022.

Interviewees differed on whether this was an issue regardless of the length of the probationary period. For example, one HR representative asserted, "I would say it's really a continuation from when we even had the one-year probationary period. It's pretty consistent that we have some supervisors that just seem to wait until the last minute," while another claimed, "I don't feel like we get the same last-minute pleas for assistance like we did when the probationary period was one year."

The interviews included several possible reasons for such delays. One was supervisors' lack of understanding about the process that even a probationary period termination requires. One of our interviewees described both supervisors' lack of knowledge and the importance of due diligence for a probationary period termination as follows:

> If I had a dollar for every time a supervisor called me with days or only a few weeks left in somebody's probationary period and wanted to fire them, I could have retired five years ago. Because they think we can just fire them like that. No evidence, no due process of any kind, no nothing, just, "Go on, you're fired." And that's not necessarily true. I would also say supervisors don't understand the ramifications other than federal agency appeal rights. They don't understand how EEO plays into it. They don't understand how unemployment compensation plays into it, and how we have to defend our actions with unemployment offices in every state.

In a related vein, another HR representative regarded a termination a day or two before the end of a probationary period as potentially "messy." In some instances, this may be because the probationary employee received positive performance feedback earlier in his or her term, as we found in our in-depth look at removal cases. An additional reason that interviewees offered is that some supervisors want to give an individual as much of an opportunity as possible to meet expectations. This may especially be the case if the job was hard to fill from the get-go or the organization invested a lot of resources in training the probationary employee. Finally, another possible reason for a late action is that supervisors lose sight of probationary period end dates. As we discuss further in the "Supervisor Notification" section later in this chapter, supervisors are not always notified about upcoming probationary period end dates and not all of them are adept at tracking when those dates are nearing.

Our statistical analysis does not appear to support the premise that many terminations were occurring at the end of the probationary period for covered personnel. As shown in Table 2.1, the average timing of a termination was 12.42 months, and 52 percent of terminations occurred during the first year. It is possible that there were pockets of later terminations, or that some of the late actions were for individuals with a probationary period shorter than two years due to prior creditable federal service.

Process-Related Concerns

In this section, we describe three additional concerns related to how the probationary period has been used. We took a process-oriented view of the probationary period from the point of hiring, when the SF-50 form was created, through the point of termination, and discuss these issues to pinpoint DoD's efforts to improve how it uses this final stage in the hiring process.

Probationary Period Calculation

As we noted earlier in this report, the length of an individual's probationary period can vary for several reasons, including prior creditable federal service and veterans preference. At the start of an individual's new SES or competitive service appointment, an SF-50 form is completed that includes the date that his or her probationary period will end. This information is important not only for the probationary period end date but also how far along an individual is in his or her probationary period can affect whether the individual meets the definition of an employee, to what level of due process her or she is entitled, and what avenues of appeal are available. We heard in interviews that HR specialists and supervisors at times do not fully understand this issue, which means sometimes there are errors on SF-50 forms and individuals are terminated as probationary employees when in reality they are past probation. HR specialists from two different military services described this problem as follows:

> I know from experience that there are a lot of SF-50s that are inaccurate. Because how does that information get coded on the SF-50? Well, some staffing specialist somewhere looks at an employee record when they're on-boarded and based on their knowledge of policy, they determine whether or not that person has to serve a probationary period. So I would say it's not uncommon at all.

> We find more SF-50 actions that are wrong in relation to the probationary period being accurate or not than we find ones that are accurate. . . . And often what happens is when they're [staffing specialists] doing that information and their files have not been really completed or provided at that point in time so they're basically, I think, just putting the canned answer that, okay, everybody gets this [date]or they get this [date]. And then when that additional information comes in often there isn't any update to the SF-50 if there's something that was reflected inaccurately from when they were first brought onboard. I would say it's probably a pretty large issue. . . . Very frequently when we've been working with our [termination] actions, if we didn't look at the SF-50 and go do our research as LMER specialists to make sure they are actually on probation, or for how long they're on probationary period for, we would have probably lost a lot of cases [appeals] for, basically, due process violations. Or basically removing someone who was not probationary, they actually had [employee] status. And we've had that happen more often than what we'd like.

This possibility of this type of error—and the serious nature of its consequences—is part of the reason for the pre-termination review described earlier. One of the steps in that process is to ensure that the individual a supervisor has flagged for termination is indeed still in his or her probationary period.

Supervisor Notification

Interviewees were at times critical about supervisors not being aware of probationary period end dates. One interviewee told us this resulted in personnel incorrectly terminated as probationary employees and later reinstated because they did not receive the due process to which they were entitled:

> We've also seen a couple of situations where the managers aren't great at keeping track of when the probation is over and they've lost track of the final probationary date. The individuals actually passed through their probationary date. And then they [supervisors] would have had to have PIP'd [prepared a Performance Improvement Plan for] the individual. We've gotten their job back because management hasn't kept track of the date and they've treated somebody as a probationer when they're actually not.

Although this is a long-standing concern, noted in a 2015 GAO report and in later research,[4] DoD is still not consistently providing supervisors with advance notice that one of their subordinates is approaching the end of his or her probationary period. Our interviews revealed there is considerable variation in this area. On a positive note, in some organizations, this information is pushed to supervisors. For example, interviewees from the Army mentioned a notification system that generates supervisor emails and Fourth Estate representatives described instances in which local HR specialists prepared reports for supervisors or used other means to communicate that a probationary period was ending soon. In other cases, it was still completely

---

[4] See Goldenkoff, 2015; and Werber, et al., 2018.

incumbent on the supervisor to pull that information on his or her own, either by referring to SF-50s directly or accessing an internal HR database, such as the Navy's Total Workforce Management System. Some of the supervisors with whom we spoke had a system in place to do this but did not think it was efficient or sufficient. As one of them explained:

> I think people who are linked to their employees should get a notification 30/60/90 days out and whether they are a veteran. My staff is linked to me in DCPDS [Defense Civilian Personnel Data System] through MyBiz. There is no reason why they can't send me an electronic notice that someone's probationary period is ending in six months. As a practitioner, we can pull the information out of the same system [but] that is not part of our function.

Notification of Appeal Rights

A final process-related concern we observed emerged from our in-depth review of removal case files. Specifically, we noted cross-case inconsistencies related to the appeal rights granted to probationary employees. Although every Navy probationary employee termination we reviewed included MSPB, OSC, and EEO appeal rights, Army, Air Force and Fourth Estate cases did not always cover all three types of rights. Furthermore, there was confusion and discrepancy in the explanation of some appeal rights. Some termination letters, which do not provide EEO appeal rights, nevertheless stated that, if the employee alleges that the discharge was based on MSPB–appropriate grounds of political affiliation or marital status, the individual may also raise issues of discrimination due to race, color, religious, sex, national origin, physical handicap, or age.

Promising Practices

Although Section 1102 of the FY 2020 NDAA calls for an analysis of best practices related to the use of the probationary period, we did not find evidence that any of DoD's practices meet the definition of the term *best practice*.[5] However, we identified practices that could be regarded as promising or innovative[6] and thus may be candidates for broader use. The first promising practice is the aforementioned push notification of probationary period end dates to supervisors. The practice may be more efficient when it is automated, which was the case in one Army example that we learned about in our interviews. However, when the notification comes from an HR specialist, as was the practice in part of the Fourth Estate, the effort also provides an opportunity for a more-personalized, proactive check-in with the supervisor.

---

[5] For example, Defense Acquisition University defines best practice as "one that has been generally accepted for producing results that are superior to those achieved by other means or because it has become a standard way of doing things—e.g., of complying with legal or ethical requirements" (Craig M. Arndt, "Using Industry Best Practices to Improve Acquisition," *Defense Acquisition Magazine*, blog post, June 20, 2018). Another source defines best practice as "a method or technique that has been proven to help organizations reach high levels of efficiency or effectiveness and produce successful outcomes. Best practices are evidence-based and proven effective through objective and comprehensive research and evaluation" (Compassion Capital Fund National Resource Center, *Strengthening Nonprofits: Capacity Builder's Resource Library. Identifying and Promoting Effective Practices*, Washington, D.C.: U.S. Department of Health and Human Services, 2010, p. 5).

[6] According to Compassion Capital Fund National Resource Center, 2010, p. 5,

> Promising practice: a method or technique that has been shown to work effectively and produce successful outcomes. Promising practices are supported, to some degree, by subjective data (e.g., interviews and anecdotal reports from the individuals implementing the practice) and objective data (e.g., feedback from subject-matter experts and the results of external audits). However, promising practices are not validated through the same rigorous research and evaluation as best practices.

> Innovative practice: a method, technique, or activity that has worked within one organization and shows promise during its early stages for becoming a promising or best practice with long-term, sustainable impact. Innovative practices must have some objective basis for claiming effectiveness and must have the potential for replication among other organizations.

If a performance or conduct issue arises, our in-depth review of cases revealed two promising practices related to documentation. First, we found that contemporaneous accounts of the incident(s) that led to termination were part of some case files. The most common version was the memorandum for record, a document written by supervisors or coworkers, usually within a day or two of an incident, that consist of a short narrative of the incident, the date, and a signature. Some files contained one such memorandum, while others had several. Memoranda for record may not be necessary or appropriate in every situation. For example, when an employee is terminated for missing production targets over a long period of time, there is no incident to report. In many, if not most situations, however, such memoranda are helpful. They can be useful for supervisors to bolster their arguments in support of termination if pushed back upon. These contemporaneous reports are particularly strong evidence that the reason for termination stated in the memorandum of termination was indeed the real reason for termination, which is useful in the case of an MSPB, OSC, or EEO appeal. These can also be useful for probationary employees to better understand why they were terminated, and perhaps to support their requests for review or appeals if pursued. When included in the case file, these memoranda also make it much easier for external parties to understand the details of the case.

Another promising documentation-related practice is when the supervisor seeks input or approval from leadership, legal, or HR prior to termination, and documents this input in the case file. In some situations, the reason for termination might be so cut-and-dry that formal approval is unnecessary. In many instances, however, approval, often in the form of a brief email, adds to the basis for termination and improves the case file. As with the memorandum for record, including the correspondence also helps bolster assertions that the termination was for the proclaimed reason.

Should a termination be deemed necessary by a supervisor, the termination checklist used in at least one Fourth Estate agency may be a helpful tool especially for a supervisor with limited experience terminating someone in their probationary period. The interviewee who cited this practice described it as follows:

> We developed a checklist to use to make sure we evaluated everything when we were doing a probationary action. Number one on the checklist is "Did you consult with HR to make sure the employee is truly probationary?" then "Is the employee truly trained to standard for performance?" For conduct, "Have you counseled the employee orally or written and/or issues any letters of warning?" We would have access to the letters of warning since we draft them and put them in our system. For counseling, we wouldn't necessarily know about that. Another of the questions is, "Has the employee indicated to you that he is experiencing any medical or personal issues? If so, has the management told the employee about EAP [Employee Assistance Program] or the reasonable accommodation process?" We want to make sure we don't miss something. If the probationary employee has a lot of personal issues, we let them know we have an employee assistance program in place. If the probationary employee says he has a hard time coming to work because he has chronic back pain, did we let the probationary employee know we have reasonable accommodations in place? Did we fulfill all of our obligations before we would terminate that employee if they were AWOL?

Finally, should a probationary period termination come to pass, another promising practice is the right for the terminated individual to request review, as the U.S. Air Force provided in the case reviewed, or the right to reply to a proposed termination. It appears that for these cases, supervisors were continuing to follow protocols outlined in Air Force Instruction 36-1001, in terms of offering the within-the-chain-of-command review option, despite that no longer being a requirement.[7] The instruction specifically stated that "at the

---

[7]   Air Force Instruction 36-1001 was superseded by DoD Instruction 1400.25, Vol. 431. However, the DoD instruction does not include guidance explicitly about probationary employees, nor does Air Force Instruction 36-1002, an Air Force-specific supplement to the DoD instruction (see Air Force Instruction 36-1001, Personnel, Managing the Civilian Performance Program, Washington, D.C.: Department of the Air Force, July 1, 1999; Air Force Instruction 36-1002, Personnel, Performance Management and Appraisal Program Administration in the Air Force, Washington, D.C.: Department of the Air Force,

probationer's request, the reviewing official determines if the action is arbitrary, capricious, or unreasonable in view of the documentation and other information provided by the supervisor relative to required performance, conduct, behavior, and attitude. The probationer receives notice in writing of the reviewing official's decision."[8]

These methods for providing the probationary employee recourse within the agency chain of command are less formal than the external appeals mechanisms and are not narrowly constrained in terms of what basis the employee may request a review of their termination. For example, a U.S. Air Force probationary employee submitted a four-page letter outlining why he thought his termination was unfair. He included a Memorandum of Concern written by his supervisor in his request. The response from the Director of Staff was sent to the employee 14 days after his request was submitted and consisted of a brief two paragraphs explaining that the termination action was appropriate and should be upheld. This mechanism, and others like it, provides the terminated probationary employee with a quick way to seek redress likely at a lower cost to DoD than an EEO or MSPB appeal. For management, the short deadline (three, five, or seven days in the cases we reviewed) and quick turnaround means the termination action is not significantly delayed.

Perceived Impact on Recruiting, Career Development, and Retention

Given congressional interest in how the probationary period has affected DoD's recruiting, development, and retention of civilian personnel, these effects were frequent topics of discussion in our interviews, with 24 interviews coded as addressing this issue. Interviewees tended to believe that the probationary period (in particular, the longer amount of time) did not have an influence on recruiting or retention. Although they were also asked about career development and training, none of the interviewees addressed that aspect of workforce management in their replies.

Those who talked about recruiting had not seen the probationary period as a deterrent for the job candidates they encountered. This was viewed at least, in part, because the desire to work for DoD was overriding concerns about probation, should they exist. As one DoD HR professional explained:

> I really haven't heard anything that that has been a concern in relation to employees, whether or not they're going to take a job with the government or they're going to stay in the job. I've often found that we have so many applicants trying to get into the government . . that I think it's just an afterthought. Whether or not they even really understand the probationary period, a lot of employees are just happy to get onboard and feel confident that they can make it work to meet the expectations.

Looking at retention, interviewees again said they tended to feel there was no effect, instead mentioning other factors, such as pay, location, and better opportunities as influencing the decision to remain at DoD:

> [W]hat affected retention the most was location, pay, moving incentives, and unwillingness to allow telework. Nobody ever brought up probation.

> Most people who leave left for greener pastures, not because of probation. In the beginning here, it was a lower GS [General Service] rating. It was a job to get a foot in the federal system and they were looking for

---

November 15, 2016; and DoD Instruction 1400.25, Volume 431, *DOD Civilian Personnel Management System: Performance Management and Appraisal Program*, Washington, D.C: U.S. Department of Defense, effective February 4, 2016, incorporating Change 3, last updated January 10, 2022).

[8]   Air Force Instruction 36-1001, 1999, p. 14.

the next step on day one. Now they are hired on the GS rating, and they seem to stay a lot longer. It is a foot in the door. No one's ever left saying it is because the probationary period is too long.

Some DoD representatives also questioned the fit or the motive of a job candidate who was concerned about the probationary period and expressed such sentiments as the following:

> I don't think it hurts in recruiting or retention at all, because that person who is worried about their probationary period might not be the right person for you in the first place.

> If you're turning down a position solely based on the length of time you're going to serve in a probationary period, that's going to send off warning flags to me. Because if you're looking for a shorter probationary period, to me that would make me question, okay, are you just going to be on your best behavior for that length of time and then once it's over, we're going to start having issues?

In contrast, union representatives said that being on probation was a concern for personnel, possibly affecting their career decisions when the labor market was tight. One interviewee also suggested that the extended probationary period might make DoD a less attractive employer than other federal agencies:

> DoD has the two-year probation but other [federal] areas don't. DoD also has a severe deficiency in cyber workers. . . . They're doing everything they can in their minds to hire people with these skillsets, but they're ignoring an elephant in the room, that, if I have two work opportunities available to me, one is with DoD that's under a two-year probationary period and then another one is with, I don't know, NOAA [National Oceanic and Atmospheric Administration], [then] I'm going to pick the one with the one-year probation over the two-year probation if everything else is set equal.

All these views may have some validity and accordingly warrant further investigation. Collecting information from prospective job applicants and job candidates who were extended a DoD employment offer would help determine how much of a decision factor the probationary period is for potential new hires. Similarly, exit surveys or other efforts to obtain feedback from departing personnel could help corroborate or refute views, such as those shared earlier about how a long probationary period affects retention.

A final career outcome-related observation that came up in the interviews pertains to retention of a specific group—specifically, individuals with disabilities who are Schedule A new hires. As we noted in Chapter Three, individuals with a disability had a higher probability of termination during their probationary period than those without a known disability. One interviewee suggested a possible explanation for this outcome: the amount of time it takes for them to receive the accommodations they need to carry out their job responsibilities. As he explains in the remarks that follow, it could mean most if not all of the individual's probationary period passes without having those accommodations in place:

> I think individuals in Schedule A hiring with targeted disabilities, they've taken it on the chin. Agencies in general are pretty reluctant to give people the accommodations that they need. I mean, I can't tell you the amount of reasonable accommodation cases I had to process in six years. . . . And if the accommodations processing takes 12 to 18 months, you're close to the end of the probation before they've even gotten their accommodation. And without that accommodation, individuals with targeted disabilities are likely to be performing at a lower rate than the other coworkers that don't have those targeted disabilities. And then that, of course, allows the agency to then say, "Oh, this isn't working out. Sorry." They terminate the individual even though, arguably, they haven't provided their accommodations under the law.

Perceived Benefits of the Extra Probationary Time

In all our interviews, we asked participants to discuss perceived benefits or advantages to DoD of the additional year of probation that the FY 2016 NDAA brought about for the department. With one exception, the interviewees identified a benefit they thought DoD could or already did enjoy. One general benefit of the extra time was that it provided new hires with additional time for training. Some interviewees felt that by the second year, individuals are "doing more hands-on work" or getting into "the meat they're going to be doing in their job." This could be not only the result of completing training, but also, as one interviewee noted, the point at which an individual finally receives his or her security clearance and could carry out the main responsibilities for which he or she was hired.

Another perceived advantage of the extra time was that it was sufficient time for a new hire to show his or her true self. Along those lines, during interviews we heard such comments as, "Anyone can keep their act together for a year, but for somebody who is a troublemaker or hard to get along with, it will show in the second year" and "I think people can maintain a certain standard of behavior for a year but after that they start flipping."

In other cases, interviewees mentioned specific contexts in which the additional probationary period offered clear benefits. One interviewee felt that his remote location was hard for new hires to adjust to and appreciated having more than a year to evaluate their performance. Another talked about how individuals coming over from the private sector needed more time to learn the ropes of working within the federal government. Others focused on a different type of employee, the new college graduate, and mentioned such programs as Pathways and New Professionals as developmental opportunities for new hires that benefited from the extended probationary period.

Finally, some interviewees felt that certain occupations, those with extensive initial training or a long work cycle, such as the research and development cycle, budget cycle, or the policy/legislative time, required the additional probationary time to truly gauge whether a new hire was a good fit for the position. When asked for specific examples, interviewees cited a wide variety of positions, including medical, scientist, engineer, program manager, HR, nuclear welding, nuclear submarine production, security, and fire. Our statistical analysis offers partial support for their opinions: Some of these occupations (specifically, Fire Protection and Prevention, HR Management, and Security Administrator) fall into the MCO/non-STEM group that we included in our regression analysis and found to have a higher probability of probationary period termination after the first year than the non-MCO/non-STEM occupation group. Future looks at the use of the probationary period and the possible value of an extended probationary period could look more closely at these occupations and others perceived as needing more time. Given what is included in administrative personnel data files, it would also be feasible to assess probationary period terminations in certain locations based on LPA and for participants in new college graduate programs.

CHAPTER SIX

Conclusion and Recommendations

In our time frame of interest, November 26, 2015, through December 31, 2020, DoD removed few individuals during their probationary periods—just 2.1 percent of covered personnel, those with new appointments to SES or competitive service. After controlling for observable factors, we found that Black personnel, those with a disability, and those in positions covered by bargaining units had a higher probability of termination than White personnel, those without a known disability, and those not in such positions, respectively. Our analysis was not causal, so it is not clear whether the extended probationary period is the primary explanation for these outcomes, if one at all. The lack of reliable performance ratings data and the dearth of appeals data provided by DoD EEO offices also limited our ability to understand why these associations were present in the data.

Looking more closely at how the extended probationary time was used, although just about half of probationary period terminations occurred after the first year, we did not observe many statistically significant patterns related to a higher probability of termination after the first year. Somewhat surprisingly, even occupations cited as especially in need of extra time for evaluation, such as engineers and scientists, were not significantly associated with a higher probability of termination during the second year of probation.

Overall, we are unable to conclude whether the extension of the probationary period from one year to two years for covered personnel was beneficial to DoD or detrimental to DoD personnel—although it was perceived as both by different interviewees. As noted at the start of the report, we were unable to access the data needed to identify the types of personnel with a higher likelihood of probationary period termination when the probationary period was one year for those with new SES or competitive service appointments. This type of analysis would have helped us to evaluate whether the extended probation was working as intended (i.e., by giving supervisors more time to assess employees whose jobs required that additional time) and to consider whether the aforementioned protected classes had a higher likelihood of probationary period termination even when the probation length was one year. Finally, the extended probationary period was in effect for a relatively short period, and DoD did not announce this change internally until ten months after it went into effect.[1] The delayed announcement suggests that supervisors had less time to learn about the extended time and gain experience using it. To truly understand how a longer probationary period influences recruiting, career development, and retention, analysis over a longer time frame—and, ideally, with perspectives of employees included—is needed.

It is important to note another possible benefit of the second year that we did not examine in this study: whether the extra year of probation enabled some probationary employees to turn around their performances or conduct and thereby avoid termination. Given the costs and time required to hire quality personnel, averted terminations are another important outcome to examine in an assessment of changes in probationary period length.

---

[1] As mentioned in Chapter One, the DoD memorandum announcing the probationary period length change was issued September 27, 2016, about ten months after the date it went into effect on November 26, 2015.

Turning our attention to implementation of the probationary period (i.e., process instead of outcomes), our analysis also revealed areas of concern and opportunities for improvement as the department continues to use the probationary period in the final stage of the hiring process. Specifically, supervisors sometimes failed to convey concerns about performance or conduct to those in their probationary periods, waiting until a termination action was initiated to bring them to the probationary employee's attention. Another perceived supervisor shortcoming—one not supported by our statistical analysis—was a tendency to wait until the probationary period was close to ending before removing the probationary employee. However, we did not find evidence that supervisors were abusing their discretion with respect to probationary periods. On the contrary, we learned about efforts to ensure that terminations were occurring for appropriate reasons, such as legal and HR reviews.

Other process-related problems pertained to calculating new hires' probationary period end dates, a computation that could be somewhat complicated when individuals have creditable federal service. We also learned that a long-standing issue (not notifying supervisors of upcoming probationary period end dates) was still a concern in parts of DoD, although interviews suggest the Army has a notification process in place in at least some locations. A third process issue apparent from our in-depth case review was that when an individual was terminated during the probationary period, the documentation provided to him or her did not consistently and accurately describe all appeal rights available.

We also note positive aspects of the extended probationary period and promising practices that may be candidates for broader application across the department. Interviewees felt that the extra year was especially useful given how long security clearances can take to obtain and in certain situations, such as for someone new to federal government work (e.g., new college graduate, more senior person with private sector work experience). The second year was regarded as when individuals get to the heart or meat of their work and their true character becomes apparent. Promising practices include different types of push notifications to supervisors; documentation of feedback to probationary employees and interactions with HR or leadership prior to initiating a termination action; and, should a termination be necessary, the use of a termination checklist and providing the terminated individual with an easy, expedient way to request a review.

Recommendations

The following recommendations are largely intended for DoD, to help it understand better termination patterns that may be problematic and to improve its use of the probationary period as an extension of the hiring process. Given the decentralized nature with which HR matters are handled within the department, a combination of organizations, including DCPAS; the ODEI; and service or component-level organizations (e.g., U.S. Army Civilian Human Resources Agency, Department of the Navy Office of Civilian Human Resources), will need to be involved in considering and implementing them.

Investigate Higher Termination Rates for Protected Classes

Our analysis of patterns in terminations indicated that Black personnel and those with a disability had a higher probability of termination than White personnel and those without a known disability, respectively. We also found that at the department level, DoD was unable to track EEO appeals initiated by employees terminated during their probationary periods. Especially in light of DoD's commitment to make the department "a workplace of choice that is characterized by diversity, equality, and inclusion,"[2] it is critical that DoD

---

[2] The department's full diversity, equity, and inclusion statement and a list of related initiatives are available online (see DoD, ODEI, undated).

develop, communicate, and implement plans to investigate why these patterns exist and to address situations in which terminations do not appear to have been for valid reasons. This effort should involve key diversity, equity, and inclusion stakeholders and be as transparent as possible, bearing in mind the need to protect the privacy of terminated individuals and those who initiated EEO appeals. Although union membership is not covered by the federal discrimination laws that EEOC enforces, there may be legal benefits to also examining why members of bargaining units had a higher probability of probationary period terminations. In that case, the involvement of unions with rights to participate in a process of this nature would help ensure that this review is perceived as fair and transparent.

Conduct Additional Research to Understand the Benefits and Shortcomings of a Longer Probationary Period

To fully assess the impact of a longer probationary period, DoD should build on the work conducted as part of this study with additional quantitative and qualitative research. As noted at the start of this chapter, analysis of probationary period terminations (and disciplinary actions) before the standard length was adjusted from one year to two years could identify what changed due to the extended time. In addition, although Congress scaled the probationary period back to one year at the end of 2022, up until that point there are seven years' worth of terminations data (2016 through 2022) to examine. A look over a longer time frame will not only provide insights about how the extended time influenced retention but will also show whether the termination patterns we found in our analysis persist over time.

We also recommend several lines of inquiry focused on the second year of probation. First, although we did not find that occupations viewed as needing more time for evaluation (e.g., those with extensive training investments or a long project work cycle) had a higher probability of termination during the second year, it is possible that with additional years of terminations data, second-year terminations for such occupations may emerge as statistically more likely. Another way to consider the benefits of the second year of probation would be to explore the "averted termination" idea. This would entail reviewing instances in which a probationary employee was either counseled or notified of pending termination and then had time while still on probation to improve. It is unclear whether DoD maintains the records needed to facilitate this type of analysis, so an exploration of the feasibility of this effort may be a necessary first step. Finally, we found in our in-depth review of cases that in some second-year terminations, supervisors appeared to be building a case for termination, with multiple documented feedback sessions and evidence of poor performance or misconduct. Although there may be benefits to this measured approach, such as avoiding litigation or appeals, it is also possible that the time spent accumulating extra documentation makes DoD less agile than it should be in removing poor performers. Accordingly, examining the relationship between termination timing, termination reasons, the extent of documentation, and outcomes (e.g., appeals and overturned terminations) may help DoD ensure that process burdens do not outweigh benefits.

Another type of research to consider is collecting information from the employee's perspective. Surveys and interviews with a sufficient number of such personnel require completion of licensing and approval processes that were beyond the scope of this study. However, gathering employees' perspectives could have much value. For example, surveying new hires and those who turned down DoD employment could be a way to gauge whether the probationary period influences decisions to join the DoD workforce. In another example, interviews with attorneys representing DoD personnel in wrongful termination actions could provide insights on abuses of discretion. This was called for in Section 1102—however, in addition to the sensitivities associated with identifying terminated personnel who pursued legal actions, these interviews also require approvals that were beyond the scope of this study.

Finally, although Congress' decision to repeal the two-year probationary period for SES and competitive service appointments makes it difficult to assess the benefits of a longer probationary period after 2022, there are still several STRL personnel demonstration projects with longer probationary periods for certain pay plans or occupations, such as scientists and engineers. DoD should consider taking a closer look at the experience of these demonstration projects to understand how often probationary period terminations within the second or third year of employment occur, whom they entailed, and why they were deemed necessary. This exercise could enable the department to present to Congress a compelling business case for restoring the longer probationary period, at least in specific contexts. It may also yield useful practices that could address the process concerns we observed in our qualitative assessment.

Improve Performance Ratings Recordkeeping

Although the probationary period is intended to facilitate removing poor performers without an overly burdensome process, problems with performance ratings in the administrative personnel data files prevented us from considering whether there was a statistically significant relationship between poor performance and termination (or disciplinary action). Specifically, many records were missing data and there was a lack of variation (i.e., few low performers) among the records with performance ratings. As DoD improves its approach to performance management and invests in the data systems that support it, ensuring performance ratings are entered into individual records for later retrieval and analysis will help ensure that DoD is effectively addressing the problem of poor employee performance, during the probationary period and later in an individual's tenure.

Increase the Accuracy of Probationary Period End Date Computations

HR professionals told us that probationary period end date computation errors happened at a troublesome level, which could mean that individuals who had completed their probationary period were terminated without the due process to which they were entitled. This in turn could have serious consequences for DoD, and accordingly, the department should take steps to understand and eliminate the reasons for such errors. It may be that an end date should not be calculated without all of a new hire's entire paperwork or perhaps these computations should be handled at a more central location by individuals who routinely perform these calculations. Concurrent with efforts to minimize such computational errors, the department could also audit or spot check SF-50s for new hires to verify the accuracy of probationary period end dates and to possibly pinpoint situations where such errors are more likely.

Use Push Notifications to Remind Supervisors of Probationary Period End Dates

Some felt supervisors failed to take appropriate termination actions in a timely manner because they lost sight of when one of their employee's probation was coming to an end. Pushing out this information, either via an automated notification system or a more personal notification from HR, is one way to reduce the likelihood of this happening. Parts of DoD are providing such notification now, demonstrating both its feasibility and usefulness.

Consider Broader Application of Termination Promising Practices

We learned about several ways to strengthen and streamline the process for terminating someone in their probationary period that are candidates for broader use. One is to document performance and conduct problems as they arise, including any related feedback provided by the supervisor. The documentation can be basic—even perhaps something recorded with a smartphone or using Microsoft Teams' record feature and then transcribed later. Such contemporaneous accounts can help support the appropriateness of the termination action and stave off accusations that the probationary employee received no prior warning of shortcomings.

Another useful practice, especially because terminations are a rare event for many supervisors, is to develop and share a termination checklist. Even if supervisors received training on probationary period actions, a simple checklist could serve as a useful memory aid for them. One possibility might be to share the checklist in conjunction with the aforementioned push notification of an upcoming probation end date.

A third practice that could be used more extensively is the Air Force's practice of providing probationary employees with an internal avenue for review of a pending termination action. A simple process with minimal documentation requirements provides the individual with a quick, low-cost way to seek redress. For management, a short timeline and expedient turnaround means the termination action is not significantly delayed. The current use of this practice within part of DoD may serve as a model.

These practices help ensure that the reason for termination is transparent and valid, and by offering additional recourse to the individual being terminated, may also improve perceptions of fairness.

Look to the Private Sector for Promising Practices Related to Termination

Although private sector employees do not have the same employment protections that individuals working within the civil service do after completing their probationary period, some private sector companies have processes in place to ensure terminations are for an appropriate reason. This is in recognition of the cost of hiring and replacing certain individuals, the impact that bad faith terminations could have on recruiting and retention, the costs of responding to an EEO appeal or termination lawsuit, and limitations to at-will employment imposed by some states. Regarding this last point, the majority of U.S. states have at least one of three common exceptions to at-will employment: the public policy exception, which forbids terminating employees in violation of well-established state policy; the implied contract exception, which bans termination after the supervisor has done something to imply a specific term of employment or an indefinite term, and the covenant of good faith and fair dealing, which prohibits terminations motivated by malice or otherwise in bad faith.[3] Accordingly, private sector firms, particularly ones with a large, diverse workforce and multiple locations, may be a source of useful ideas for handling poor performers, especially when it is apparent they cannot or will not improve and termination is the best course of action for the organization.

---

[3]   For a discussion of these exceptions, see Charles J. Muhl, "The Employment-At-Will Doctrine: Three Major Exceptions," *Monthly Labor Review*, Vol. 124, 2001; and Legal Information Institute, "Employment-at-Will Doctrine," webpage, undated.

Statistical Analysis Detail

This appendix provides additional details about the data set we used for our statistical analysis, including how we constructed the data set, how we identified populations of interest; how we measured terminations, disciplinary actions, and demographics; and our regression models. Throughout the appendix, we note decisions and assumptions that influenced our analysis.

Data Set

We received APF Civilian Transaction Personnel Files from the DMDC for FY 2015 through FY 2020. Select variables from the December 2020 Civilian Transaction Personnel File that RAND receives routinely through DRS 85000 were appended to these FYs. The combination provided us with complete transaction records for individuals from November 26, 2015, through December 31, 2020. We dropped personnel actions associated with dates outside October 1, 2015, through December 31, 2020. This involved pulling all unique scrambled Social Security numbers from these files between FY 2015 and calendar year 2020.

Approach to Identifying Populations of Interest

This part of our analysis consisted of filtering personnel based on appointment types and NOA codes, addressing cases in which individuals had multiple appointments, and setting a probationary period end date.

First, we only kept records associated with the following appointment types:

- Competitive Service
    – Appointment type 1A (Competitive—Career)
    – Appointment type 2A (Competitive—Career Conditional)
- SES
    – Appointment type 5A (SES—Career)

Following that, we flagged appointments based on the following NOA codes:

- Competitive Service
    – NOA 100 (Career Appointment)
    – NOA 101 (Career-Conditional Appointment)
    – NOA 140 (Reinstatement-Career)
    – NOA 141 (Reinstatement-Career-Conditional)
    – NOA 500 (Conversion to Career Appointment)
    – NOA 501 (Conversion to Career-Conditional Appointment)
    – NOA 540 (Conversion to Reinstatement-Career)
    – NOA 541 (Conversion to Reinstatement-Career-Conditional)

- SES
    - NOA 142 (SES Career Appointment)
    - NOA 542 (Conversion to SES Career Appointment)

Going through this process yielded 164,694 personnel with a new competitive service appointment and 275 personnel with a new SES appointment. Given the relatively small number of SES appointments,[1] moving forward with our analysis we opted to combine the personnel with either a new competitive service appointment or SES appointment for a total of 164,969 personnel covered by Section 1599e of 10 U.S.C. After completing this process, we found that of the personnel retained, 16,592 personnel with new appointments in the covered time frame had multiple appointments during that window. We opted to keep the first appointment for those individuals.

Our next step was to set a probationary period end date for all personnel. We accomplished this by setting a two-year probation based on first appointment. We were aware that actual probationary period lengths could vary, typically being shorter due to creditable federal service or longer due to inclusion in certain STRL personnel demonstration projects.[2] To consider how many personnel might have a shorter probationary period, we estimated personnel with possible prior federal service by identifying individuals in our data file who were newly appointed during our covered time frame, had a prior appointment with a break between that appointment and the one focused on in our analysis of no more than 30 days, *and* both of those appointments were with the same agency. We did not—and could not—consider whether work was similar across appointments, so this could be considered a high-end estimate.[3] We found that 6,432 (3.9 percent) of personnel newly appointed to a competitive service/SES position during the covered time frame had a prior appointment with the same agency with a break in service of no more than 30 days.

Turning our attention to STRL, estimating the number of newly-appointed personnel with a three-year probationary period was more challenging because it required a review of Federal Register Notices and internal operating guidance, and in some cases only subsets of personnel within a specific STRL (e.g., scientists and engineers) were subject to a longer probationary period. In addition, the internal operating guidance was unavailable for some STRL projects (e.g., U.S. Army labs) and we found that some pay plans were used across STRLs that had varying policies regarding probationary period length (i.e., we could not assume those pay plans had a set probationary period length due to this variation). A final complication was that some of the STRLs with a three-year probationary period did not uniformly apply that longer period on new hires with veterans' preference.

Overall, we estimated that 13,052 of the 164,969 personnel newly appointed to a competitive service/SES position during the covered time frame (7.9 percent) were in an STRL project based on their pay plan. This includes the following:

---

[1] We made this decision given the both the desire to minimize the possibility of identification via inference for this small group and the low likelihood of obtaining statistically significant results when analyzing personnel with SES appointments independently. Given the results of our statistical analysis (e.g., Black personnel and those with disabilities more likely to be terminated during their probationary period), it may be worthwhile in future research to tease out differences between newly appointed competitive service and SES personnel.

[2] We focused on STRL demonstration projects because at the time of our study, the Civilian Acquisition Workforce Personnel Demonstration Project, also known as AcqDemo, did not have a longer probationary period for any occupational series.

[3] According to 5 CFR Section 315.802, prior federal civilian service counts toward completion of a probationary period when the prior service meets three conditions: (1) is in the same agency, (2) is in the same line of work (based on the individual's actual duties and responsibilities); and (3) contains or is followed by no more than one break in service no more than 30 calendar days (see 5 CFR Section 315.802, Length of Probationary Period; Crediting Service).

1. 5,399 people (3.3 percent of personnel newly appointed to a competitive service/SES position) in STRL Scientist and Engineer pay plans: Some portion of this group, but not all, have a three-year probationary period. As noted above, the precise number is not readily determined because sometimes even within a pay plan the length varies across STRLs (e.g., for the ND pay plan, scientists and engineers in the Naval Information Warfare Center had a three-year probationary period but those in Naval Sea Systems Warfare Center had a two-year pay period).
2. 479 people (0.3 percent) in General Support pay plans: Our review of guidance suggests all these personnel have a two-year probationary period.
3. 7,174 people (4.3 percent) in other pay plans, such as Administrative, Professional, and Technician: Again, there is variation within these pay plans regarding the probationary period length, and sometimes even within the same pay plan when different STRLs making use of the same pay plan differ in their operating guidance.

It is reasonable to assume that fewer than 12,573 personnel (13,052 covered personnel in an STRL project minus the 479 General Support pay plan personnel), or fewer than 7.6 percent, out of the 164,969 covered personnel in the time frame of interest had a three-year probationary period. This is a relatively small share of the total group, and given overall study resources, the original study timeline, and the small number of observed terminations (discussed in the next section), the team decided not to conduct the extensive research necessary to pinpoint the actual number of personnel with a three-year probationary period. Finer-grained analysis would require obtaining from the military services the internal operating guidance for various STRLs, exploring the intersection of pay plan and agency within our data file, and accounting for veterans' preference.

After completing these two exploratory exercises, one related to the potential of creditable federal service and one related to the potential of a longer probationary period, we opted to proceed with the original plan of setting all covered personnel with a two-year probationary period based on their first appointment.

Approach to Measuring Terminations and Disciplinary Actions

Terminations from Civil Service

For covered personnel (those with new competitive service or SES appointments during the covered time frame) we used NOA code 385, "Termination During Probation or Trial Period" as the basis for calculating terminations from civil service during a probationary or trial period. Using data through December 2020 for all those personnel, we found 14 individuals who were terminated twice, often within a short window of time (e.g., a few days), and with no record of a new appointment in between terminations. We assumed these were data entry errors or duplications of some sort and counted only the first termination. We also revisited the issue of multiple appointments noted earlier in this appendix. Of the 164,969 people within our analysis time frame, 3,492 had a probationary period termination action (based on NOA code 385) recorded after their first appointment (but before subsequent appointments); 292 people had a probationary period termination action recorded either before their first appointment or after their second or later appointment; 14 were terminated twice for the same appointment (two terminations after their first appointment with no new appointment in between); resulting in a total of 3,798 termination actions recorded in the data set in the time frame of interest; and 202,626161,477 were not terminated (among first appointment records). Ultimately, we included in our analysis of terminations first appointment terminations for 3,492 competitive service/SES personnel (2.1 percent of all those in their probationary period).

Disciplinary Actions

Although supervisors have a wide variety of disciplinary actions at their disposal in the event of poor employee performance or misconduct, very few of them are recorded consistently in the DMDC civilian personnel files we used for our analysis. Specifically, we used two measures of suspensions in our analysis: NOA code 450, "Suspension-Not-to-Exceed [date]" and NOA Code 452, "Suspension-Indefinite." Using these two measures, we found that 1,304 competitive service/SES personnel (0.8 percent of all those in their probationary period) were subject to disciplinary actions.

Demographic Measures of Interest

In addition to personal attributes of those in their probationary or trial periods, such as age, gender, race, ethnicity, veteran status, disability status, and level of education attained, we also considered in our analysis organizational and occupational characteristics such as agency, whether one was in a bargaining unit, whether one was in a large occupation or MCO, supervisory status, pay grade at appointment, and LPA. Additional details about the variables we selected and any transformations we executed (e.g., creation of bins or categories) follow. We also discuss why we were unable to include performance ratings in our analysis.

- **Age:** After determining the number of personnel terminated and those disciplined were relatively small and considering different ways to analyze age, we decided to use the "Year of Birth" variable to create two categories, (1) younger than age 40 and (2) age 40 and older. We chose this split because the Age Discrimination in Employment Act of 1967 forbids age discrimination against people who are age 40 or older.[4]
- **Gender:** Categories include male and female.
- **Race:** Race categories include White, Black, Asian, American Indian or Alaska Native, Hawaiian/Pacific Islander, and Other Race.
- **Ethnicity:** The variable for ethnicity identifier indicates whether an individual is Hispanic or Latino.
- **Veteran status:** The variable for veteran status reflected different eras of military service. We regarded an individual as a veteran if his or her coded as one of the following four categories: veteran, era unknown; pre-Vietnam-era veteran; Vietnam-era veteran; or post-Vietnam-era veteran.
- **Disability status:** The disability variable within the DMDC data files includes a long list of types of disabilities and serious health conditions. We regarded an individual as having a disability or serious health condition unless his or her record was coded as "I do not have a disability or serious health condition" or unknown.
- **Education level:** We used the education level variable to create four categories: no college (high school graduate or certificate of equivalency, terminal occupational program, or less); some college (less than one year of college, one year of college, two years of college, associate degree, three years of college, or four years of college no bachelor's degree); bachelor's degree (bachelor's degree or post-bachelor's); and graduate degree (first professional, master's degree, doctorate, or post-doctorate)
- **Pay grade at appointment:** We used the same pay grade binning approach employed in an earlier report to classify entry-level, mid-level, or senior-level personnel.[5] We also created a separate bin for SES-level personnel. The earlier binning approach did not cover WG personnel. We opted to categorize WG levels

---

[4] 29 U.S.C. Section 631, Age Limits, January 3, 2016.

[5] The full binning approach is discussed on page 7 of Guo, Partyka, and Gates, 2014.

1 through 5 as entry-level personnel, 6 through 10 as mid-level personnel, and 11 through 15 as senior-level personnel.

- **Bargaining unit:** The bargaining unit variable includes a list of specific units. All values were coded as "yes, in bargaining unit" except for the two cases of "no, not in bargaining unit," codes 7777 and 8888.
- **Supervisory status:** The supervisory status variable includes different categories of leaders, including supervisor, manager, supervisor (Civil Service Reform Act), Management Official (Civil Service Reform Act), leader, and team leader, all of which we treated as "yes, has supervisory status," in our analysis.
- **LPA:** This measure is intended to capture geographic differences in local labor markets, attitudes toward employment rights, and relative costs of labor and other inputs. We included the six largest LPAs in our models, which each include at least 2 percent of covered personnel.

Organizational Membership

We looked at organizational membership in two ways. First, we included in our analysis whether someone was in the Air Force, Army, Navy, or Fourth Estate. Second, given the potential for variation in policy and procedure at a lower echelon of organization, we also include subagencies within our analysis. Specifically, we used the Agency-Subelement variable in our data set, which included 163 total subagencies. Cognizant of the small numbers of terminations and disciplinary actions among our populations and limits on how many variables we could include in our regression models, we opted to focus on the subagencies that included at least 1 percent of our group of covered personnel in their probationary period (1,650 people) and grouped the remaining organizations into an all others category. That narrowed the group of subagencies down to 27 organizations, which together included 127,191 (77 percent) of covered personnel. A list of those subagencies is provided in Table A.1.

Occupation

We also considered occupation in several ways. First, similar to our approach for organizational subagencies, we opted to focus on occupations (at the four-digit OPM occupation code level, e.g., 1102–Contracting) that included at least 1 percent of covered personnel. This resulted in a set of 23 occupations, which together included 65,547 (40 percent) of covered personnel. Table A.2 features a list of those occupations, organized along the "PATCOB" (Professional/Administrative/Technical/Other White Collar/Blue Collar) dimensions.

After reviewing results of preliminary analysis with our sponsor, we were encouraged to also consider MCOs and whether there were patterns in terminations or disciplinary actions related to those occupations. To facilitate this additional line of inquiry, our sponsor provided us with two DoD lists of MCOs that our sponsor provided, one from FY 2015 and the other from FY 2020. We coded an occupation as an MCO if it was included on either of those lists. We also opted to consider personnel working in STEM occupations, using a 2012 DoD STEM occupational taxonomy developed by the DoD STEM Executive Board. The occupations that are both MCO and STEM are listed in Table A.3, and Table A.4 includes the MCOs that are not STEM. Note there is some overlap between the largest occupations (Table A.2) and the MCOs. For example, IT Management, Nursing, and Economist are larger occupations in terms of their share of covered personnel and are also MCO/STEM occupations. Similarly, the HR Management and Police occupations are both larger occupations and MCO/non-STEM. As we will discuss further in the next section, this overlap led us to explore the relationship between occupation and terminations in different ways within our regression models.

TABLE A.1

DoD Subagencies Included in Statistical Analysis

Air Force

Air Combat Cmd

Air Educ and Training Cmd

Air National Guard Units (Title 32)

Headquarters, USAF Reserve Cmd

USAF Civilian Career Training

USAF Materiel Cmd

Army

Army National Guard Units (Title 32)

Field Operating Offices, Office of the Secretary of the Army

U.S. Army Corps of Engineers

U.S. Army Installation Mgmt Cmd

U.S. Army Medical Cmd

U.S. Army Reserve Cmd

Navy

Naval Air Systems Cmd

Naval Educ and Training Cmd

Naval Facilities Engineering Cmd

Naval Medical Cmd

Naval Sea Systems Cmd

Navy Installations Cmd

Space and Naval Warfare Sys Cmd

U.S. Fleet Forces Cmd

U.S. Marine Corps

U.S. Pacific Fleet

Fourth Estate

Defense Commissary Agency

Defense Contract Mgmt Agency

Defense Finance and Accounting Svcs

Defense Logistics Agency

DoD Education Activity

SOURCE: Authors' analysis of DMDC data.

NOTES: The organizations in this list each include at least 1 percent of covered personnel. Cmd = Command; Educ = Education; Mgmt = Management; Svcs = Services; Sys = Systems; USAF = U.S. Air Force.

TABLE A.2

Four-Digit Level OPM Occupations Included in Statistical Analysis

Professional

    Contracting

    Economist

    Mechanical Engineering

Administrative

    Financial Admin and Program

    HR Mgmt

    IT Mgmt

    Logistics Mgmt

    Mgmt and Program Analysis

    Misc Admin and Program

    Security Admin

Technical

    General Business and Industry

    Sports Specialist

Clerical

    HR Assistance

    Misc Clerk and Assistant

    Sales Store Clerical

Other White Collar

    Nurse

    Police

    Security Guard

Blue Collar

    Aircraft Mechanic

    Misc Warehousing and Stock Handling

SOURCE: Authors' analysis of DMDC data.

NOTES: The occupations in this list each include at least 1 percent of covered personnel. The DMDC data included three additional occupations with at least 1 percent of covered personnel: occupation codes 0034 ("blankocc2"), 0008 ("institutionaladmin"), and 0221 ("positionclassification"). We were unable to obtain definitive labels for these occupations. Admin = Administration; Cmd = Command; Mgmt = Management; Misc = Miscellaneous; Svcs = Services; USAF = U.S. Air Force.

TABLE A.3
MCO/STEM Occupations

Occupation
Computer Engineering
Computer Science
Dental Officer
Economist
Electronic Engineering
Foreign Affairs
Intelligence
International Relations
IT Mgmt
Logistics Mgmt
Medical Officer
Nuclear Engineering
Nurse
Pharmacist
Physician's Assistant
Practical Nurse
Psychology
Safety Engineering

SOURCE: DoD MCO FY 2015 and FY 2020 lists.
NOTE: Mgmt = Management.

Performance Ratings

Because the probationary period is a time for supervisors to pay close attention to the performance of newly appointed personnel and to take action to address poor performance, assessing the relationship between performance ratings and terminations and other disciplinary actions could provide useful information about whether the probationary period was being used as intended. However, past research has noted problems with performance ratings in DMDC data, such as a large amount of missing data, different rating scales for individuals on different pay plans, and a lack of variation in ratings (e.g., very few personnel receiving a "fail" or otherwise unsatisfactory score).[6] We still opted to take a look at performance ratings in the hope that some of these issues had improved in recent years. Unfortunately, we encountered some of the same issues, especially with respect to missing data: roughly 60 percent of observations were unusable. Even when we focused on covered personnel part of the DOD Performance Management and Appraisal Program, which places greater emphasis on performance feedback, we still found a similar number of observations with unusable

---

[6]   One example of research that encountered these issues is Jennifer Lamping Lewis, Laura Werber, Cameron Wright, Irina Elena Danescu, Jessica Hwang, and Lindsay Daugherty, *2016 Assessment of the Civilian Acquisition Workforce Personnel Demonstration Project*, Santa Monica, Calif.: RAND Corporation, RR-1783-OSD, 2017.

TABLE A.4
MCO/Non-STEM Occupations

Occupation
Accounting
Administrative Officer
Auditing
Budget Analysis
Contracting
Criminal Investigating
Educ and Training Technician
Educ and Vocational Training
Explosives Safety
Financial Admin and Program
Fire Protection and Prevention
General Educ and Training
General Supply
HR Mgmt
Inventory Mgmt
Language Specialist
Physical Therapist
Police
Production Control
Public Affairs
Quality Assurance
Safety and Occupational Health Mgmt
Security Admin
Social Work
Telecommunications
Traffic Mgmt
Training Instruction
Transportation Specialist

SOURCE: DoD MCO FY 2015 and FY 2020 lists.

NOTE: Admin = Administration; Educ = Education; Mgmt = Management.

ratings.[7] The issue of few low performers was also present again: Less than 1 percent of covered personnel had a rating of less than fully successful.[8] For these reasons, we were unable to include performance ratings in our assessment of termination and disciplinary action distribution patterns.

Regression Analysis

Approach

To identify patterns related to terminations and disciplinary actions, we used regression analysis. Regression analysis enables us to control for multiple factors at once, which is important because we have good reason to suspect that the factors themselves are also related to our measures of interest: probability of termination during the probationary period, probability of termination after the first year of probation, and probability of disciplinary action during the probationary period. The binary nature of these dependent variables meant that probit regression was the appropriate technique to employ. We report marginal effects, which tells us a variable's effect on the probability of termination, disciplinary action, or termination timing depending on the model.

In the regression models, we control for (i.e., consider) the demographic measures described in the preceding section. As we noted in the previous section, we examined the influence of occupational membership in multiple ways. First, we considered four groups of occupations using the MCO/STEM occupation lists: MCO/STEM, MCO/non-STEM, non-MCO/STEM, and non-MCO/non-STEM. In our second model, we retained three of those groups—MCO/STEM, non-MCO/STEM, and non-MCO/non-STEM—and included as separate variables all the specific occupations that constitute the MCOl/non-STEM group (those in Table A.4). We opted for this approach because after running additional models in which each MCO and STEM grouping was disaggregated (i.e., each occupation was a distinct variable), we found that there was enough variation in non-STEM/MCOs to warrant presenting their marginal effects separately. For our third model, we included as separate variables the occupations with at least 1 percent of the covered personnel (those in Table A.2).

All of the independent variables in our model are categorical, which requires that we specify and exclude a referent group. That is, our results are expressed as differences from the referent group. Table A.5 lists the referent groups for each independent variable. For variables that pertain to protected classes (e.g., gender, race, ethnicity, age, veteran status, and disability status) the referent group is the nonprotected class. For other variables, the referent group was chosen somewhat more arbitrarily, but typically we used a smaller group as the referent. In each case, the referent group is a decision we made that can be changed. However, when we shared preliminary results with the sponsor in a project update, the sponsor was satisfied with our choice of referent groups and the implications that had for interpreting the results.

Results

Table 3.1 provided a summary of the variables included in our regression models. We ran all three models for three dependent variables: probability of termination during the probationary period, probability of disciplinary action during the probationary period, and probability of termination after the first year of probation (conditional on being terminated).

---

[7]   We regarded observations coded as "not rated" or "exclusion" as unusable and looked at observations at both six months and 12 months after a new appointment.

[8]   On a five-point scale, *less than fully successful* means either unacceptable or between successful and unacceptable.

TABLE A.5

Referent Groups for Regression Models

Groups
Age: younger than age 40
Gender: male
Race: White
Ethnicity: non-Hispanic
Veteran status: non-veteran
Disability status: no known disability
Education: no college (i.e., high school diploma or less)
Pay grade at appointment: entry-level
Bargaining unit: not in a bargaining unit
Supervisory status: not a supervisor
LPA: all other LPAs (including the rest of the United States)
Agency: Fourth Estate
Subagency: all other subagencies
Occupation Model 1: MCO/STEM
Occupation Model 2: non-MCO/non-STEM
Occupation Model 3: all other occupations

The full set of regression models, including those with the excepted service appointment comparison group, are provided in Tables A.6 to A.14. Specifically, Tables A.6 to A.8 include the results of our analysis of the probability of termination during the probationary period, Tables A.9 to A.11 include the results of our analysis of the probability of disciplinary action during the probationary period, and Tables A.12 to A.14 include the results of our analysis of probability of termination after the first year of probation. To facilitate interpretation and application of our result, we report our results (the coefficients) as marginal effects (i.e., how much more likely a specific category of personnel is to be terminated or disciplined compared with the referent group) all else equal.

TABLE A.6

Regression Model 1: Probability of Termination During Probationary Period, MCO/STEM Occupation Group Specification

Variable	Coefficient (marginal effect)	p-Value
Age		
Age 40 and older	−0.002	0.031
Gender		
Female	−0.006	0.000
Missing	—	—
Race		
Black	0.011	0.000
Asian	−0.004	0.026
American Indian or Alaska Native	0.012	0.000
Hawaiian/Pacific Islander	−0.006	0.143
Other	0.006	0.001
Missing	0.003	0.357
Ethnicity		
Hispanic	−0.004	0.041
Missing	—	—
Veteran		
Yes	−0.006	0.000
Missing	—	—
Disability status		
Yes	0.005	0.000
Unknown	0.009	0.074
Education		
Some college	−0.005	0.000
Bachelor's degree or higher	−0.008	0.000
Missing	—	—
Pay grade at appointment		
Mid-level	−0.006	0.000
Senior-level	−0.011	0.000
SES level	−0.018	0.272
Missing	−0.002	0.343
Bargaining unit		
In bargaining unit	0.004	0.000
Missing	−0.011	0.362

Table A.6—Continued

Variable	Coefficient (marginal effect)	p-Value
Supervisor status		
Yes	−0.003	0.191
Missing	—	—
LPA		
Washington, D.C.	−0.001	0.662
Seattle/Tacoma	0.003	0.112
San Diego	0.004	0.060
Los Angeles	−0.003	0.193
Boston	0.003	0.205
Hawaii	−0.010	0.000
Not in an LPA	−0.005	0.118
Missing	−0.002	0.086
Service/component		
Air Force	−0.013	0.000
Army	−0.005	0.035
Navy	−0.009	0.004
Missing	−0.022	0.179
Subagency		
Air Force		
Air Combat Cmd	0.009	0.016
Air Educ and Training Cmd	0.005	0.140
Air National Guard Units (Title 32)	—	—
Headquarters, USAF Reserve Cmd	−0.003	0.405
USAF Civilian Career Training	0.000	0.947
USAF Materiel Cmd	0.009	0.000
Army		
Army National Guard Units (Title 32)	−0.030	0.002
Field Operating Offices, Office of the Secretary of the Army	−0.013	0.151
U.S. Army Corps of Engineers	0.007	0.002
U.S. Army Installation Mgmt Cmd	0.004	0.067
U.S. Army Medical Cmd	0.012	0.000
U.S. Army Reserve Cmd	0.013	0.000

Table A.6—Continued

Variable	Coefficient (marginal effect)	p-Value
Navy		
Naval Air Systems Cmd	0.007	0.015
Naval Educ and Training Cmd	0.006	0.194
Naval Facilities Engineering Cmd	0.011	0.001
Naval Medical Cmd	0.021	0.000
Naval Sea Systems Cmd	−0.006	0.075
Navy Installations Cmd	0.014	0.000
Space and Naval Warfare Sys Cmd	−0.002	0.662
U.S. Fleet Forces Cmd	0.011	0.000
U.S. Marine Corps	0.010	0.003
U.S. Pacific Fleet	0.017	0.000
Fourth Estate		
Defense Commissary Agency	0.006	0.019
Defense Contract Mgmt Agency	−0.009	0.025
Defense Finance and Accounting Svcs	−0.002	0.519
Defense Logistics Agency	0.002	0.350
DoD Education Activity	0.018	0.009
Occupation group		
MCO/STEM	−0.004	0.001
MCO/non-STEM	−0.007	0.000
Non-MCO/STEM	−0.009	0.000
Observations	164,345	
Pseudo-R^2	0.047	

SOURCE: Authors' analysis of DMDC data.

NOTES: A dash indicates that there is no coefficient. Cmd = Command; Mgmt = Management; Sys = System; USAF = U.S. Air Force.

TABLE A.7

Regression Model 2: Probability of Termination During Probationary Period, MCO/Non-STEM Occupation Group Breakout Specification

Variable	Coefficient (marginal effect)	p-Value
Age		
Age 40 and older	−0.002	0.027
Gender		
Female	−0.006	0.000
Missing	—	—
Race		
Black	0.011	0.000
Asian	−0.004	0.026
American Indian or Alaska Native	0.012	0.000
Hawaiian/Pacific Islander	−0.006	0.144
Other	0.006	0.002
Missing	0.003	0.327
Ethnicity		
Hispanic	−0.004	0.035
Missing	—	—
Veteran		
Yes	−0.006	0.000
Missing	—	—
Disability status		
Yes	0.005	0.000
Unknown	0.009	0.074
Education		
Some college	−0.005	0.000
Bachelor's degree or higher	−0.008	0.000
Missing	—	—
Pay grade at appointment		
Mid-level	−0.006	0.000
Senior-level	−0.011	0.000
SES level	−0.018	0.275
Missing	−0.002	0.306
Bargaining unit		
In bargaining unit	0.003	0.000
Missing	−0.012	0.341

Table A.7—Continued

Variable	Coefficient (marginal effect)	p-Value
Supervisor status		
Yes	−0.003	0.161
Missing	—	—
LPA		
Washington, D.C.	−0.001	0.699
Seattle/Tacoma	0.003	0.103
San Diego	0.004	0.062
Los Angeles	−0.004	0.180
Boston	0.003	0.191
Hawaii	−0.010	0.000
Not in an LPA	−0.005	0.118
Missing	−0.001	0.124
Service/component		
Air Force	−0.012	0.000
Army	−0.005	0.058
Navy	−0.008	0.009
Missing	−0.022	0.187
Subagency		
Air Force		
Air Combat Cmd	0.009	0.019
Air Educ and Training Cmd	0.005	0.186
Air National Guard Units (Title 32)	—	—
Headquarters, USAF Reserve Cmd	−0.004	0.366
USAF Civilian Career Training	0.001	0.895
USAF Materiel Cmd	0.009	0.000
Army		
Army National Guard Units (Title 32)	−0.030	0.002
Field Operating Offices, Office of the Secretary of the Army	−0.012	0.161
U.S. Army Corps of Engineers	0.007	0.002
U.S. Army Installation Mgmt Cmd	0.004	0.063
U.S. Army Medical Cmd	0.012	0.000
U.S. Army Reserve Cmd	0.013	0.000

Table A.7—Continued

Variable	Coefficient (marginal effect)	p-Value
Navy		
Naval Air Systems Cmd	0.006	0.027
Naval Educ and Training Cmd	0.005	0.229
Naval Facilities Engineering Cmd	0.011	0.001
Naval Medical Cmd	0.021	0.000
Naval Sea Systems Cmd	−0.007	0.049
Navy Installations Cmd	0.013	0.000
Space and Naval Warfare Sys Cmd	−0.003	0.595
U.S. Fleet Forces Cmd	0.011	0.000
U.S. Marine Corps	0.009	0.007
U.S. Pacific Fleet	0.017	0.000
Fourth Estate		
Defense Commissary Agency	0.006	0.020
Defense Contract Mgmt Agency	−0.009	0.036
Defense Finance and Accounting Svcs	−0.003	0.341
Defense Logistics Agency	0.003	0.308
DoD Education Activity	0.017	0.013
Occupation group		
MCO/STEM	−0.004	0.001
Non-MCO/STEM	−0.009	0.000
MCO/non-STEM occupations		
Accounting	0.012	0.018
Administrative Officer	0.006	0.586
Auditing	−0.004	0.444
Budget Analysis	−0.013	0.077
Contracting	−0.009	0.002
Criminal Investigating	0.010	0.616
Educ and Training Technician	−0.018	0.020
Educ and Vocational Training	—	—
Explosives Safety	—	—
Financial Admin and Program	−0.012	0.007
Fire Protection and Prevention	−0.021	0.000
General Educ and Training	0.014	0.134
General Supply	−0.007	0.356

Table A.7—Continued

Variable	Coefficient (marginal effect)	p-Value
HR Mgmt	−0.012	0.018
Inventory Mgmt	−0.022	0.078
Language Specialist	—	—
Physical Therapist	−0.006	0.638
Police	0.001	0.765
Production Control	−0.003	0.701
Public Affairs	0.002	0.810
Quality Assurance	−0.003	0.553
Safety and Occ Health Mgmt	−0.008	0.165
Security Admin	−0.013	0.003
Social Work	0.001	0.938
Telecommunications	−0.021	0.083
Traffic Mgmt	−0.016	0.379
Training Instruction	−0.002	0.725
Transportation Specialist	—	—
Observations	164,161	
Pseudo-R^2	0.0486	

SOURCE: Authors' analysis of DMDC data.

NOTE: A dash indicates that there is no coefficient. Admin = Administration; Cmd = Command; Educ = Education; Eng = Engineering; Mgmt = Management; Misc = Miscellaneous; Occ = Occupation; USAF = U.S. Air Forces.

TABLE A.8

Regression Model 3: Probability of Termination During Probationary Period, Occupations with at Least 1 Percent of Probationers Specification

Variable	Coefficient (marginal effect)	p-Value
Age		
Age 40 and older	−0.001	0.102
Gender		
Female	−0.006	0.000
Missing	—	—
Race		
Black	0.011	0.000
Asian	−0.004	0.020
American Indian or Alaska Native	0.012	0.000
Hawaiian/Pacific Islander	−0.005	0.150
Other	0.006	0.002
Missing	0.003	0.336
Ethnicity		
Hispanic	−0.004	0.032
Missing	—	—
Veteran		
Yes	−0.006	0.000
Missing	—	—
Disability status		
Yes	0.005	0.000
Unknown	0.010	0.055
Education		
Some college	−0.006	0.000
Bachelor's degree or higher	−0.009	0.000
Missing	—	—
Pay grade at appointment		
Mid-level	−0.007	0.000
Senior-level	−0.011	0.000
SES level	−0.017	0.292
Missing	−0.001	0.531
Bargaining unit		
In bargaining unit	0.004	0.000
Missing	−0.011	0.359

Table A.8—Continued

Variable	Coefficient (marginal effect)	p-Value
Supervisor status		
Yes	−0.002	0.294
Missing	—	—
LPA		
Washington, D.C.	−0.001	0.503
Seattle/Tacoma	0.004	0.070
San Diego	0.004	0.060
Los Angeles	−0.004	0.147
Boston	0.004	0.111
Hawaii	−0.010	0.000
Not in an LPA	−0.004	0.167
Missing	0.001	0.370
Service/component		
Air Force	−0.012	0.000
Army	−0.004	0.086
Navy	−0.008	0.009
Missing	−0.019	0.263
Subagency		
Air Force		
Air Combat Cmd	0.009	0.022
Air Educ and Training Cmd	0.004	0.216
Air National Guard Units (Title 32)	—	—
Headquarters, USAF Reserve Cmd	−0.003	0.429
USAF Civilian Career Training	0.003	0.559
USAF Materiel Cmd	0.010	0.000
Army		
Army National Guard Units (Title 32)	−0.031	0.001
Field Operating Offices, Office of the Secretary of the Army	−0.013	0.123
U.S. Army Corps of Engineers	0.005	0.016
U.S. Army Installation Mgmt Cmd	0.003	0.270
U.S. Army Medical Cmd	0.010	0.000
U.S. Army Reserve Cmd	0.015	0.000

Table A.8—Continued

Variable	Coefficient (marginal effect)	p-Value
Navy		
Naval Air Systems Cmd	0.007	0.024
Naval Educ and Training Cmd	0.007	0.106
Naval Facilities Engineering Cmd	0.011	0.001
Naval Medical Cmd	0.020	0.000
Naval Sea Systems Cmd	−0.007	0.034
Navy Installations Cmd	0.012	0.001
Space and Naval Warfare Sys Cmd	−0.004	0.485
U.S. Fleet Forces Cmd	0.010	0.000
U.S. Marine Corps	0.009	0.006
U.S. Pacific Fleet	0.017	0.000
Fourth Estate		
Defense Commissary Agency	0.009	0.001
Defense Contract Mgmt Agency	−0.008	0.032
Defense Finance and Accounting Svcs	−0.001	0.715
Defense Logistics Agency	0.001	0.613
DoD Education Activity	0.019	0.005
Occupations with at least 1 percent of those in probationary period		
Professional		
Contracting	−0.007	0.015
Economist	−0.009	0.006
Mechanical Eng	−0.014	0.001
Administrative		
Financial Admin and Program	−0.011	0.018
HR Mgmt	−0.011	0.035
IT Mgmt	−0.002	0.287
Logistics Mgmt	−0.015	0.001
Mgmt and Program Analysis	−0.006	0.132
Misc Admin and Program	−0.004	0.172
Security Admin	−0.013	0.004
Technical		
General Business and Industry	−0.018	0.000
Sports Specialist	−0.005	0.081

Table A.8—Continued

Variable	Coefficient (marginal effect)	p-Value
Clerical		
HR Assistance	0.005	0.144
Misc Clerk and Assistant	−0.005	0.029
Sales Store Clerical	−0.005	0.117
Other White Collar		
Nurse	0.006	0.028
Police	0.002	0.374
Security Guard	0.004	0.115
Blue Collar		
Aircraft Mechanic	0.004	0.233
Misc Warehousing and Stock Handling	0.007	0.015
Unnamed occupations		
1.institutionaladmin	−0.002	0.463
1.blankocc2	−0.015	0.001
1.positionclassification	−0.011	0.012
Observations	164,345	
Pseudo-R^2	0.049	

SOURCE: Authors' analysis of DMDC data.

NOTE: A dash indicates that there is no coefficient. Admin = Administration; Cmd = Command; Educ = Education; Eng = Engineering; Mgmt = Management; Misc = Miscellaneous; Occ = Occupation; USAF = U.S. Air Forces.

TABLE A.9

Regression Model 1: Probability of Disciplinary Action During Probationary Period, MCO/ STEM Occupation Group Specification

Variable	Coefficient (marginal effect)	p-Value
Age		
Age 40 and older	0.000	0.319
Gender		
Female	−0.004	0.000
Missing	—	—
Race		
Black	0.002	0.000
Asian	0.000	0.938
American Indian or Alaska Native	0.003	0.055
Hawaiian/Pacific Islander	−0.002	0.462
Other	0.002	0.117
Missing	0.005	0.004
Ethnicity		
Hispanic	−0.002	0.133
Missing	—	—
Veteran		
Yes	0.001	0.121
Missing	—	—
Disability status		
Yes	0.000	0.716
Unknown	−0.002	0.560
Education		
Some college	0.000	0.444
Bachelor's degree or higher	−0.006	0.000
Missing	—	—
Pay grade at appointment		
Mid-level	0.001	0.106
Senior-level	−0.001	0.423
SES level	—	—
Missing	0.001	0.298
Bargaining unit		
In bargaining unit	0.001	0.028
Missing	0.007	0.251

Table A.9—Continued

Variable	Coefficient (marginal effect)	p-Value
Supervisor status		
Yes	0.002	0.024
Missing	—	—
LPA		
Washington, D.C.	0.002	0.077
Seattle/Tacoma	0.000	0.886
San Diego	0.000	0.904
Los Angeles	−0.001	0.487
Boston	0.003	0.034
Hawaii	−0.001	0.725
Not in an LPA	−0.002	0.306
Missing	0.004	0.000
Service/component		
Air Force	−0.002	0.250
Army	0.001	0.614
Navy	0.000	0.883
Missing	0.013	0.001
Subagency		
Air Force		
Air Combat Cmd	0.000	0.909
Air Educ and Training Cmd	0.001	0.715
Air National Guard Units (Title 32)	0.001	0.772
Headquarters, USAF Reserve Cmd	−0.002	0.248
USAF Civilian Career Training	−0.005	0.246
USAF Materiel Cmd	0.006	0.000
Army		
Army National Guard Units (Title 32)	−0.002	0.478
Field Operating Offices, Office of the Secretary of the Army	−0.003	0.496
U.S. Army Corps of Engineers	0.000	0.878
U.S. Army Installation Mgmt Cmd	0.001	0.491
U.S. Army Medical Cmd	−0.001	0.583
U.S. Army Reserve Cmd	0.003	0.022

Table A.9—Continued

Variable	Coefficient (marginal effect)	p-Value
U.S. Navy		
Naval Air Systems Cmd	0.001	0.579
Naval Educ and Training Cmd	0.005	0.055
Naval Facilities Engineering Cmd	−0.003	0.203
Naval Medical Cmd	0.002	0.256
Naval Sea Systems Cmd	−0.001	0.676
Navy Installations Cmd	0.001	0.614
Space and Naval Warfare Sys Cmd	0.000	1.000
U.S. Fleet Forces Cmd	0.007	0.000
U.S. Marine Corps	−0.001	0.584
U.S. Pacific Fleet	0.004	0.036
Fourth Estate		
Defense Commissary Agency	−0.004	0.026
Defense Contract Mgmt Agency	−0.007	0.014
Defense Finance and Accounting Svcs	−0.003	0.193
Defense Logistics Agency	0.002	0.134
DoD Education Activity	0.008	0.058
Occupation group		
MCO/STEM	−0.004	0.000
MCO/non-STEM	0.000	0.788
Non-MCO/STEM	−0.005	0.000
Observations	164,555	
Pseudo-R^2	0.055	

SOURCE: Authors' analysis of DMDC data.

NOTE: A dash indicates that there is no coefficient. Admin = Administration; Cmd = Command; Educ = Education; Eng = Engineering; Mgmt = Management; Misc = Miscellaneous; Occ = Occupation; USAF = U.S. Air Forces.

TABLE A.10

Regression Model 2: Probability of Disciplinary Action During Probationary Period, MCO/Non-STEM Occupation Group Breakout Specification

Variable	Coefficient (marginal effect)	p-Value
Age		
Age 40 and older	0.000	0.320
Gender		
Female	−0.004	0.000
Missing	—	—
Race		
Black	0.002	0.000
Asian	0.000	0.918
American Indian or Alaska Native	0.003	0.056
Hawaiian/Pacific Islander	−0.002	0.462
Other	0.002	0.087
Missing	0.005	0.006
Ethnicity		
Hispanic	−0.002	0.173
Missing	—	—
Veteran		
Yes	0.001	0.134
Missing	—	—
Disability status		
Yes	0.000	0.647
Unknown	−0.002	0.553
Education		
Some college	0.000	0.429
Bachelor's degree or higher	−0.006	0.000
Missing	—	—
Pay grade at appointment		
Mid-level	0.001	0.132
Senior-level	−0.001	0.381
SES level	—	—
Missing	0.001	0.327
Bargaining unit		
In bargaining unit	0.001	0.018
Missing	0.007	0.244

Table A.10—Continued

Variable	Coefficient (marginal effect)	p-Value
Supervisor status		
Yes	0.002	0.024
Missing	—	—
LPA		
Washington, D.C.	0.002	0.089
Seattle/Tacoma	0.000	0.883
San Diego	0.000	0.842
Los Angeles	−0.001	0.513
Boston	0.003	0.037
Hawaii	−0.001	0.721
Not in an LPA	−0.002	0.326
Missing	0.004	0.000
Service/component		
Air Force	−0.003	0.155
Army	0.000	0.876
Navy	0.000	0.860
Missing	0.013	0.002
Subagency		
Air Force		
Air Combat Cmd	0.000	0.902
Air Educ and Training Cmd	0.001	0.660
Air National Guard Units (Title 32)	0.001	0.774
Headquarters, USAF Reserve Cmd	−0.002	0.260
USAF Civilian Career Training	−0.006	0.206
USAF Materiel Cmd	0.006	0.000
Army		
Army National Guard Units (Title 32)	−0.002	0.473
Field Operating Offices, Office of the Secretary of the Army	−0.003	0.559
U.S. Army Corps of Engineers	0.000	0.787
U.S. Army Installation Mgmt Cmd	0.001	0.408
U.S. Army Medical Cmd	0.000	0.733
U.S. Army Reserve Cmd	0.003	0.024

Table A.10—Continued

Variable	Coefficient (marginal effect)	p-Value
Navy		
Naval Air Systems Cmd	0.001	0.462
Naval Educ and Training Cmd	0.005	0.047
Naval Facilities Engineering Cmd	−0.002	0.239
Naval Medical Cmd	0.002	0.220
Naval Sea Systems Cmd	−0.001	0.762
Navy Installations Cmd	0.001	0.463
Space and Naval Warfare Sys Cmd	0.000	0.958
U.S. Fleet Forces Cmd	0.007	0.000
U.S. Marine Corps	−0.001	0.663
U.S. Pacific Fleet	0.004	0.029
Fourth Estate		
Defense Commissary Agency	−0.005	0.015
Defense Contract Mgmt Agency	−0.007	0.011
Defense Finance and Accounting Svcs	−0.003	0.180
Defense Logistics Agency	0.002	0.278
DoD Education Activity	0.007	0.085
Occupation group		
MCO/STEM	−0.004	0.000
Non-MCO/STEM	−0.005	0.000
MCO/non-STEM occupations		
Accounting	—	—
Administrative Officer	−0.002	0.752
Auditing	−0.006	0.250
Budget Analysis	0.004	0.129
Contracting	0.001	0.535
Criminal Investigating	0.009	0.299
Educ and Training Technician	0.002	0.485
Educ and Vocational Training	—	—
Explosives Safety	—	—
Financial Admin and Program	0.001	0.674
Fire Protection and Prevention	−0.002	0.468
General Educ and Training	0.004	0.546
General Supply	0.001	0.804

Table A.10—Continued

Variable	Coefficient (marginal effect)	p-Value
HR Mgmt	0.005	0.010
Inventory Mgmt	0.008	0.027
Language Specialist	—	—
Physical Therapist	—	—
Police	0.000	0.937
Production Control	−0.010	0.132
Public Affairs	−0.004	0.607
Quality Assurance	−0.001	0.853
Safety and Occ Health Mgmt	−0.002	0.573
Security Admin	0.001	0.773
Social Work	—	—
Telecommunications	−0.009	0.173
Traffic Mgmt	—	—
Training Instruction	−0.002	0.636
Transportation Specialist	0.005	0.569
Observations	163,075	
Pseudo-R^2	0.0555	

SOURCE: Authors' analysis of DMDC data.

NOTE: A dash indicates that there is no coefficient. Admin = Administration; Cmd = Command; Educ = Education; Eng = Engineering; Mgmt = Management; Misc = Miscellaneous; Occ = Occupation; USAF = U.S. Air Forces.

TABLE A.11

Regression Model 3: Probability of Disciplinary Action During Probationary Period, Occupations with at Least 1 Percent of Probationers Specification

Variable	Coefficient (marginal effect)	p-Value
Age		
Age 40 and older	0.001	0.245
Gender		
Female	−0.004	0.000
Missing	—	—
Race		
Black	0.002	0.000
Asian	0.000	0.866
American Indian or Alaska Native	0.004	0.048
Hawaiian/Pacific Islander	−0.002	0.477
Other	0.002	0.094
Missing	0.005	0.005
Ethnicity		
Hispanic	−0.002	0.151
Missing	—	—
Veteran		
Yes	0.001	0.039
Missing	—	—
Disability status		
Yes	0.000	0.807
Unknown	−0.002	0.610
Education		
Some college	−0.001	0.342
Bachelor's degree or higher	−0.007	0.000
Missing	—	—
Pay grade at appointment		
Mid-level	0.001	0.351
Senior-level	−0.001	0.358
SES level	—	—
Missing	0.001	0.257

Table A.11—Continued

Variable	Coefficient (marginal effect)	p-Value
Bargaining unit		
In bargaining unit	0.001	0.020
Missing	0.007	0.259
Supervisor status		
Yes	0.002	0.021
Missing	—	—
LPA		
Washington, D.C.	0.001	0.213
Seattle/Tacoma	0.000	0.987
San Diego	0.000	0.903
Los Angeles	−0.001	0.468
Boston	0.003	0.021
Hawaii	0.000	0.791
Not in an LPA	−0.002	0.300
Missing	0.005	0.000
Service/component		
Air Force	−0.002	0.171
Army	0.001	0.715
Navy	0.000	0.929
Missing	0.015	0.000
Subagency		
Air Force		
Air Combat Cmd	0.000	0.891
Air Educ and Training Cmd	0.001	0.749
Air National Guard Units (Title 32)	0.001	0.827
Headquarters, USAF Reserve Cmd	−0.002	0.253
USAF Civilian Career Training	−0.005	0.248
USAF Materiel Cmd	0.006	0.000

Table A.11—Continued

Variable	Coefficient (marginal effect)	p-Value
Army		
Army National Guard Units (Title 32)	−0.003	0.415
Field Operating Offices, Office of the Secretary of the Army	−0.004	0.434
U.S. Army Corps of Engineers	0.000	0.742
U.S. Army Installation Mgmt Cmd	0.000	0.911
U.S. Army Medical Cmd	−0.002	0.107
U.S. Army Reserve Cmd	0.004	0.008
Navy		
Naval Air Systems Cmd	0.001	0.682
Naval Educ and Training Cmd	0.005	0.029
Naval Facilities Engineering Cmd	−0.003	0.179
Naval Medical Cmd	0.002	0.434
Naval Sea Systems Cmd	−0.001	0.455
Navy Installations Cmd	0.001	0.671
Space and Naval Warfare Sys Cmd	0.000	0.893
U.S. Fleet Forces Cmd	0.007	0.000
U.S. Marine Corps	−0.001	0.686
U.S. Pacific Fleet	0.003	0.059
Fourth Estate		
Defense Commissary Agency	−0.005	0.020
Defense Contract Mgmt Agency	−0.007	0.010
Defense Finance and Accounting Svcs	−0.003	0.159
Defense Logistics Agency	0.002	0.252
DoD Education Activity	0.007	0.064
Occupations with at least 1 percent of those in probationary period		
Professional		
Contracting	0.002	0.268
Economist	−0.006	0.006
Mechanical Eng	−0.014	0.017

Table A.11—Continued

Variable	Coefficient (marginal effect)	p-Value
Administrative		
Financial Admin and Program	0.002	0.436
HR Mgmt	0.005	0.007
IT Mgmt	−0.006	0.000
Logistics Mgmt	−0.003	0.190
Mgmt and Program Analysis	−0.003	0.203
Misc Admin and Program	0.001	0.414
Security Admin	0.001	0.773
Technical		
General Business and Industry	−0.002	0.482
Sports Specialist	−0.002	0.299
Clerical		
HR Assistance	−0.001	0.730
Misc Clerk and Assistant	−0.005	0.017
Sales Store Clerical	0.001	0.848
Other White Collar		
Nurse	0.002	0.310
Police	0.000	0.877
Security Guard	0.002	0.140
Blue Collar		
Aircraft Mechanic	0.000	0.830
Misc Warehousing and Stock Handling	0.000	0.807
Unnamed Occupations		
1.institutionaladmin	0.000	0.911
1.blankocc2	−0.004	0.026
1.positionclassification	−0.007	0.003
Observations	164,555	
Pseudo-R^2	0.057	

SOURCE: Authors' analysis of DMDC data.

NOTE: A dash indicates that there is no coefficient. Admin = Administration; Cmd = Command; Educ = Education; Eng = Engineering; Mgmt = Management; Misc = Miscellaneous; Occ = Occupation; USAF = U.S. Air Forces.

TABLE A.12

Regression Model 1: Probability of Termination After First Year of Probation, Conditional on Being Terminated, MCO/STEM Occupation Group Specification

Variable	Coefficient (marginal effect)	p-Value
Age		
Age 40 and older	−0.026	0.160
Gender		
Female	−0.005	0.821
Missing	—	—
Race		
Black	−0.025	0.226
Asian	0.059	0.173
American Indian or Alaska Native	0.018	0.770
Hawaiian/Pacific Islander	−0.014	0.881
Other	−0.081	0.051
Missing	−0.064	0.391
Ethnicity		
Hispanic	0.040	0.335
Missing	—	—
Veteran		
Yes	−0.023	0.238
Missing	—	—
Disability status		
Yes	−0.025	0.229
Unknown	0.030	0.801
Education		
Some college	0.083	0.001
Bachelor's degree or higher	0.051	0.027
Missing	—	—
Pay grade at appointment		
Mid-level	0.028	0.162
Senior-level	0.057	0.360
SES level	—	—
Missing	0.053	0.262

Table A.12—Continued

Variable	Coefficient (marginal effect)	p-Value
Bargaining unit		
In bargaining unit	−0.040	0.113
Missing	—	—
Supervisor status		
Yes	0.039	0.454
Missing	—	—
LPA		
Washington, D.C.	0.027	0.477
Seattle/Tacoma	−0.032	0.495
San Diego	−0.055	0.263
Los Angeles	−0.073	0.278
Boston	−0.040	0.495
Hawaii	0.162	0.017
Not in an LPA	0.087	0.254
Missing	−0.019	0.362
Service/component		
Air Force	0.100	0.190
Army	0.010	0.867
Navy	0.050	0.520
Missing	—	—
Subagency		
Air Force		
Air Combat Cmd	−0.147	0.134
Air Educ and Training Cmd	−0.064	0.472
Air National Guard Units (Title 32)	—	—
Headquarters, USAF Reserve Cmd	0.049	0.635
USAF Civilian Career Training	0.088	0.504
USAF Materiel Cmd	0.027	0.678

Table A.12—Continued

Variable	Coefficient (marginal effect)	p-Value
Army		
Army National Guard Units (Title 32)	—	—
Field Operating Offices, Office of the Secretary of the Army	−0.042	0.865
U.S. Army Corps of Engineers	0.022	0.686
U.S. Army Installation Mgmt Cmd	0.015	0.770
U.S. Army Medical Cmd	0.074	0.061
U.S. Army Reserve Cmd	−0.091	0.143
Navy		
Naval Air Systems Cmd	0.068	0.351
Naval Educ and Training Cmd	−0.021	0.851
Naval Facilities Engineering Cmd	0.075	0.349
Naval Medical Cmd	−0.062	0.409
Naval Sea Systems Cmd	−0.025	0.777
Navy Installations Cmd	−0.012	0.880
Space and Naval Warfare Sys Cmd	0.093	0.510
U.S. Fleet Forces Cmd	0.027	0.705
U.S. Marine Corps	0.028	0.739
U.S. Pacific Fleet	0.005	0.951
Fourth Estate		
Defense Commissary Agency	−0.160	0.009
Defense Contract Mgmt Agency	0.038	0.699
Defense Finance and Accounting Svcs	0.195	0.009
Defense Logistics Agency	0.138	0.026
DoD Education Activity	−0.370	0.028
Occupation group		
MCO/STEM	−0.019	0.546
MCO/non-STEM	0.074	0.024
Non-MCO/STEM	0.008	0.839
Observations	3,484	
Pseudo-R^2	0.039	

SOURCE: Authors' analysis of DMDC data.

NOTE: A dash indicates that there is no coefficient. Admin = Administration; Cmd = Command; Educ = Education; Eng = Engineering; Mgmt = Management; Misc = Miscellaneous; Occ = Occupation; USAF = U.S. Air Forces.

TABLE A.13

Regression Model 2: Probability of Termination After First Year of Probation, Conditional on Being Terminated, MCO/Non-STEM Occupation Group Breakout Specification

Variable	Coefficient (marginal effect)	p-Value
Age		
Age 40 and older	−0.026	0.153
Gender		
Female	−0.002	0.926
Missing	—	—
Race		
Black	−0.024	0.249
Asian	0.062	0.149
American Indian or Alaska Native	0.024	0.696
Hawaiian/Pacific Islander	−0.015	0.876
Other	−0.089	0.035
Missing	−0.065	0.389
Ethnicity		
Hispanic	0.039	0.354
Missing	—	—
Veteran		
Yes	−0.025	0.202
Missing	—	—
Disability status		
Yes	−0.026	0.220
Unknown	0.030	0.801
Education		
Some college	0.083	0.001
Bachelor's degree or higher	0.057	0.017
Missing	—	—
Pay grade at appointment		
Mid-level	0.033	0.112
Senior-level	0.068	0.278
SES level	—	—
Missing	0.054	0.247
Bargaining unit		
In bargaining unit	−0.043	0.091
Missing	—	—

Table A.13—Continued

Variable	Coefficient (marginal effect)	p-Value
Supervisor status		
Yes	0.031	0.561
Missing	—	—
LPA		
Washington, D.C.	0.037	0.328
Seattle/Tacoma	−0.029	0.534
San Diego	−0.049	0.322
Los Angeles	−0.072	0.287
Boston	−0.038	0.511
Hawaii	0.164	0.016
Not in an LPA	0.081	0.292
Missing	−0.020	0.347
Service/component		
Air Force	0.118	0.133
Army	0.037	0.561
Navy	0.087	0.286
Missing	—	—
Subagency		
Air Force		
Air Combat Cmd	−0.149	0.133
Air Educ and Training Cmd	−0.058	0.513
Air National Guard Units (Title 32)	—	—
Headquarters, USAF Reserve Cmd	0.046	0.654
USAF Civilian Career Training	0.094	0.475
USAF Materiel Cmd	0.032	0.626
Army		
Army National Guard Units (Title 32)	—	—
Field Operating Offices, Office of the Secretary of the Army	−0.076	0.758
U.S. Army Corps of Engineers	0.023	0.681
U.S. Army Installation Mgmt Cmd	0.016	0.762
U.S. Army Medical Cmd	0.076	0.059
U.S. Army Reserve Cmd	−0.091	0.141

Table A.13—Continued

Variable	Coefficient (marginal effect)	p-Value
Navy		
Naval Air Systems Cmd	0.050	0.502
Naval Educ and Training Cmd	−0.029	0.797
Naval Facilities Engineering Cmd	0.062	0.447
Naval Medical Cmd	−0.076	0.309
Naval Sea Systems Cmd	−0.037	0.677
Navy Installations Cmd	−0.032	0.702
Space and Naval Warfare Sys Cmd	0.072	0.609
U.S. Fleet Forces Cmd	0.016	0.824
U.S. Marine Corps	0.009	0.914
U.S. Pacific Fleet	−0.007	0.927
Fourth Estate		
Defense Commissary Agency	−0.132	0.040
Defense Contract Mgmt Agency	0.063	0.539
Defense Finance and Accounting Svcs	0.222	0.004
Defense Logistics Agency	0.164	0.011
DoD Education Activity	−0.343	0.051
Occupation group		
MCO/STEM	−0.024	0.433
Non-MCO/STEM	0.002	0.956
MCO/non-STEM occupations		
Accounting	0.027	0.818
Administrative Officer	0.041	0.909
Auditing	0.146	0.269
Budget Analysis	−0.174	0.402
Contracting	0.035	0.663
Criminal Investigating	—	—
Educ and Training Technician	0.214	0.304
Educ and Vocational Training	—	—
Explosives Safety	—	—
Financial Admin and Program	0.062	0.600
Fire Protection and Prevention	0.079	0.546

Table A.13—Continued

Variable	Coefficient (marginal effect)	p-Value
General Educ and Training	0.307	0.211
General Supply	−0.188	0.372
HR Mgmt	0.012	0.933
Inventory Mgmt	−0.042	0.904
Language Specialist	—	—
Physical Therapist	−0.086	0.800
Police	0.100	0.111
Production Control	0.185	0.258
Public Affairs	0.304	0.217
Quality Assurance	0.071	0.563
Safety and Occ Health Mgmt	0.105	0.479
Security Admin	0.099	0.402
Social Work	−0.316	0.089
Telecommunications	—	—
Traffic Mgmt	—	—
Training Instruction	0.175	0.232
Transportation Specialist	—	—
Observations	3,480	
Pseudo-R^2	0.0421	

SOURCE: Authors' analysis of DMDC data.

NOTE: A dash indicates that there is no coefficient. Admin = Administration; Cmd = Command; Educ = Education; Eng = Engineering; Mgmt = Management; Misc = Miscellaneous; Occ = Occupation; USAF = U.S. Air Forces.

TABLE A.14

Regression Model 3: Probability of Termination After First Year of Probation, Conditional on Being Terminated, Occupations with at Least 1 Percent of Probationers Specification

Variable	Coefficient (marginal effect)	p-Value
Age		
Age 40 and older	−0.027	0.138
Gender		
Female	−0.007	0.742
Missing	—	—
Race		
Black	−0.026	0.217
Asian	0.060	0.163
American Indian or Alaska Native	0.014	0.820
Hawaiian/Pacific Islander	−0.004	0.969
Other	−0.073	0.080
Missing	−0.066	0.374
Ethnicity		
Hispanic	0.042	0.302
Missing	—	—
Veteran		
Yes	−0.024	0.233
Missing	—	—
Disability status		
Yes	−0.031	0.148
Unknown	0.009	0.942
Education		
Some college	0.085	0.000
Bachelor's degree or higher	0.059	0.010
Missing	—	—
Pay grade at appointment		
Mid-level	0.025	0.262
Senior-level	0.054	0.386
SES level	—	—
Missing	0.046	0.324
Bargaining unit		
In bargaining unit	−0.034	0.177
Missing	—	—

Table A.14—Continued

Variable	Coefficient (marginal effect)	p-Value
Supervisor status		
Yes	0.034	0.511
Missing	—	—
LPA		
Washington, D.C.	0.025	0.517
Seattle/Tacoma	−0.037	0.426
San Diego	−0.060	0.222
Los Angeles	−0.078	0.246
Boston	−0.045	0.439
Hawaii	0.164	0.016
Not in an LPA	0.078	0.304
Missing	−0.027	0.238
Service/component		
Air Force	0.093	0.221
Army	0.002	0.975
Navy	0.047	0.555
Missing	—	—
Subagency		
Air Force		
Air Combat Cmd	−0.149	0.129
Air Educ and Training Cmd	−0.067	0.449
Air National Guard Units (Title 32)	—	—
Headquarters, USAF Reserve Cmd	0.034	0.746
USAF Civilian Career Training	0.099	0.458
USAF Materiel Cmd	0.013	0.837
Army		
Army National Guard Units (Title 32)	—	—
Field Operating Offices, Office of the Secretary of the Army	−0.043	0.863
U.S. Army Corps of Engineers	0.019	0.728
U.S. Army Installation Mgmt Cmd	0.038	0.488
U.S. Army Medical Cmd	0.062	0.137
U.S. Army Reserve Cmd	−0.129	0.044

Table A.14—Continued

Variable	Coefficient (marginal effect)	p-Value
Navy		
Naval Air Systems Cmd	0.052	0.487
Naval Educ and Training Cmd	−0.033	0.771
Naval Facilities Engineering Cmd	0.064	0.433
Naval Medical Cmd	−0.077	0.312
Naval Sea Systems Cmd	−0.022	0.805
Navy Installations Cmd	0.008	0.921
Space and Naval Warfare Sys Cmd	0.087	0.543
U.S. Fleet Forces Cmd	0.011	0.882
U.S. Marine Corps	0.021	0.808
U.S. Pacific Fleet	−0.011	0.884
Fourth Estate		
Defense Commissary Agency	−0.136	0.041
Defense Contract Mgmt Agency	0.035	0.719
Defense Finance and Accounting Svcs	0.177	0.018
Defense Logistics Agency	0.122	0.071
DoD Education Activity	−0.370	0.029
Occupations with at least 1 percent of those in probationary period		
Professional		
Contracting	0.025	0.749
Economist	−0.025	0.768
Mechanical Eng	−0.005	0.963
Administrative		
Financial Admin and Program	0.049	0.680
HR Mgmt	0.006	0.965
IT Mgmt	−0.053	0.338
Logistics Mgmt	0.348	0.016
Mgmt and Program Analysis	−0.125	0.207
Misc Admin and Program	0.089	0.231
Security Admin	0.001	0.773
Technical		
General Business and Industry	0.063	0.575
Sports Specialist	0.023	0.750

Table A.14—Continued

Variable	Coefficient (marginal effect)	p-Value
Clerical		
HR Assistance	0.041	0.598
Misc Clerk and Assistant	−0.003	0.955
Sales Store Clerical	−0.142	0.040
Other White Collar		
Nurse	−0.036	0.542
Police	0.066	0.307
Security Guard	−0.109	0.064
Blue Collar		
Aircraft Mechanic	−0.001	0.994
Misc Warehousing and Stock Handling	−0.007	0.901
Unnamed Occupations		
1.institutionaladmin	−0.113	0.135
1.blankocc2	0.008	0.950
1.positionclassification	0.004	0.970
Observations	3,484	
Pseudo-R^2	0.043	

SOURCE: Authors' analysis of DMDC data.

NOTES: A dash indicates that there is no coefficient. Admin = Administration; Cmd = Command; Educ = Education; Eng = Engineering; Mgmt = Management; Misc = Miscellaneous; USAF = U.S. Air Forces.

Abbreviations

AFGE	American Federation of Government Employees
APF	appropriated funds
AWOL	absent without official leave
DCPAS	Defense Civilian Personnel Advisory Service
DMDC	Defense Manpower Data Center
DoD	U.S. Department of Defense
EEO	Equal Employment Opportunity
EEOC	Equal Employment Opportunity Commission
FY	fiscal year
GAO	U.S. Government Accountability Office
HR	human resources
IT	information technology
LMER	Labor Management Employee Relations
LPA	Locality Pay Area
MCO	mission critical occupation
MSPB	Merit Systems Protection Board
NDAA	National Defense Authorization Act
NOA	nature of action
OPM	U.S. Office of Personnel Management
OSC	Office of Special Counsel
SES	Senior Executive Service
SF-50	Standard Form 50
STEM	science, technology, engineering, and mathematics
STRL	Science and Technology Reinvention Laboratory
WG	wage grade

References

5 CFR Section 315.802—*See* Code of Federal Regulations, Title 5, Administrative Personnel, Section 315.802, Length of Probationary Period; Crediting Service.

5 CFR Section 315.804—*See* Code of Federal Regulations, Title 5, Administrative Personnel, Section 315.804, Termination of Probationers for Unsatisfactory Performance or Conduct, last updated December 1, 2005.

5 CFR Section 315.805— *See* Code of Federal Regulations, Title 5, Administrative Personnel, Section 315.805, Termination of Probationers for Conditions Arising Before Appointment, last updated February 7, 2008.

5 U.S.C. Section 4303—*See* U. S. Code, Title 5, Government Organization and Employees, Chapter 43, Performance Appraisal, Section 4303.

5 U.S.C. Section 7513—*See* U.S. Code, Title 5, Chapter 75, Adverse Actions, Section 7513, Cause and Procedure.

10 U.S.C. Section 1599e—*See* U.S. Code, Title 10, Section 1599e, Probationary Period for Employees.

29 U.S.C. Section 631—*See* U.S. Code, Title 29, Labor, Chapter 14, Age Discrimination in Employment, Section 631, Age Limits.

Adu, Phillip, *A Step-by-Step Guide to Qualitative Data Coding*, Oxford: Routledge, 2019.

Air Force Instruction 36-1001, *Personnel, Managing the Civilian Performance Program*, Washington, D.C.: Department of the Air Force, July 1, 1999.

Air Force Instruction 36-1002, *Personnel, Performance Management and Appraisal Program Administration in the Air Force*, Washington, D.C.: Department of the Air Force, November 15, 2016.

Arndt, Craig M., "Using Industry Best Practices to Improve Acquisition," *Defense Acquisition Magazine*, blog post, June 20, 2018. As of January 14, 2022:
https://www.dau.edu/library/defense-atl/blog/Using-Industry-Best-Practices--to-Improve-Acquisition

Code of Federal Regulations, Title 5, Administrative Personnel, Section 315.802, Length of Probationary Period; Crediting Service, 1995.

Code of Federal Regulations, Title 5, Administrative Personnel, Section 315.804, Termination of Probationers for Unsatisfactory Performance or Conduct, last updated December 1, 2005.

Code of Federal Regulations, Title 5, Administrative Personnel, Section 315.805, Termination of Probationers for Conditions Arising Before Appointment, last updated February 7, 2008.

Compassion Capital Fund National Resource Center, *Strengthening Nonprofits: Capacity Builder's Resource Library. Identifying and Promoting Effective Practices*, Washington, D.C.: U.S. Department of Health and Human Services, 2010.

DeCuir-Gunby, J.T., P. L. Marshall, and A. W. McCulloch, "Developing and Using a Codebook for the Analysis of Interview Data: An Example from a Professional Development Research Project," *Field Methods*, Vol. 23, No. 2, 2011, pp. 136–155.

Department of Defense Instruction 1400.25, Volume 431, *DOD Civilian Personnel Management System: Performance Management and Appraisal Program*, Washington, D.C.: U.S. Department of Defense, effective February 4, 2016, incorporating Change 3, last updated January 10, 2022.

DoD Instruction—*See* Department of Defense Instruction.

DoD, ODEI—*See* U.S. Department of Defense, Office for Diversity, Equity, and Inclusion.

Federal Managers Association, "2021 Issue Briefs," 2021. As of January 14, 2022:
http://fedmanagers.org/fma/files/ccLibraryFiles/Filename/000000001571/2021%20FMA%20Issue%20Briefs_Final.pdf

Goldenkoff, Robert, *Federal Workforce: Improved Supervision and Better Use of Probationary Periods Are Needed to Address Substandard Employee Performance*, Washington, D.C.: U.S. Government Accountability Office, GAO-15-191, February 2015. As of January 14, 2022:
https://www.gao.gov/assets/670/668339.pdf

Guo, Christopher, Philip Hall-Partyka, and Susan M. Gates, *Retention and Promotion of High-Quality Civil Service Workers in the Department of Defense Acquisition Workforce*, Santa Monica, Calif.: RAND Corporation, RR-748-OSD, 2014. As of January 14, 2022:
https://www.rand.org/pubs/research_reports/RR748.html

Legal Information Institute, "Employment-at-Will Doctrine," webpage, undated. As of May 18, 2022:
https://www.law.cornell.edu/wex/employment-at-will_doctrine

Lewis, Jennifer Lamping, Laura Werber, Cameron Wright, Irina Elena Danescu, Jessica Hwang, and Lindsay Daugherty, *2016 Assessment of the Civilian Acquisition Workforce Personnel Demonstration Project*, Santa Monica, Calif.: RAND Corporation, RR-1783-OSD, 2017. As of January 14, 2022:
https://www.rand.org/pubs/research_reports/RR1783.html

McInnis, Kathleen J., *Defense Primer: The Department of Defense*, Washington, D.C.: Congressional Research Service, IF10543, last updated November 8, 2021. As of January 14, 2022:
https://fas.org/sgp/crs/natsec/IF10543.pdf

Miles, Matthew B., and A. Michael Huberman, *Qualitative Data Analysis: An Expanded Sourcebook*, 2nd ed., Thousand Oaks, Calif.: Sage Publications, 1994.

Muhl, Charles J., "The Employment-At-Will Doctrine: Three Major Exceptions," *Monthly Labor Review*, Vol. 124, 2001, pp. 3–11.

Office of the Assistant Secretary of Defense, Deputy Assistant Secretary of Defense for Civilian Personnel Policy, "Subject: Probationary Period for New Employees," memorandum, Washington, D.C., September 27, 2016. As of May 16, 2022:
https://www.dcpas.osd.mil/sites/default/files/2021-12/CPP%20Memo%20-%20Probationary%20Period%20 for%20New%20Employ.pdf

Public Law 114–92, National Defense Authorization Act for Fiscal Year 2016, November 25, 2015.

Public Law 116–92, National Defense Authorization Act for Fiscal Year 2020, December 20, 2019.

Saldaña, Johnny, *The Coding Manual for Qualitative Researchers*, Thousand Oaks, Calif.: Sage Publications, 2016.

U.S. Code, Title 5, Government Organization and Employees, Chapter 43, Performance Appraisal, Section 4303, Actions Based on Unacceptable Performance, January 3, 2012.

U.S. Code, Title 5, Chapter 75, Adverse Actions, Section 7513, Cause and Procedure, January 7, 2011.

U.S. Code, Title 10, Section 1599e, Probationary Period for Employees, January 6, 2017.

U.S. Code, Title 29, Labor, Chapter 14, Age Discrimination in Employment, Section 631, Age Limits, January 3, 2016.

U.S. Department of Defense, Defense Civilian Personnel Advisory Service, "Addressing Performance Issues Early," webpage, undated. As of January 5, 2022:
https://www.dcpas.osd.mil/policy/performance/dodperformancemanagementappraisal/

U.S. Department of Defense, Office for Diversity, Equity, and Inclusion, homepage, undated. As of May 15, 2022:
https://diversity.defense.gov/DoD-Diversity-and-Inclusion-Initiatives

U.S. Office of Personnel Management, "Addressing and Resolving Poor Performance: A Guide for Supervisors," March 2017. As of January 5, 2022:
https://www.opm.gov/policy-data-oversight/employee-relations/reference-materials/

U.S. Office of Personnel Management, *2019 Federal Employee Viewpoint Survey: Governmentwide Management Report*, Washington, D.C., 2019. As of January 15, 2022:
https://www.opm.gov/fevs/reports/governmentwide-reports/governmentwide-management-report/ governmentwide-report/2019/2019-governmentwide-management-report.pdf

Werber, Laura, Paul W. Mayberry, Mark Doboga, and Diana Gehlhaus, *Support for DoD Supervisors in Addressing Poor Employee Performance: A Holistic Approach*, Santa Monica, Calif.: RAND Corporation, RR-2665-OSD, 2018. As of January 14, 2022:
https://www.rand.org/pubs/research_reports/RR2665.html